THE MINES OF NEPTUNE
Minerals and Metals from the Sea

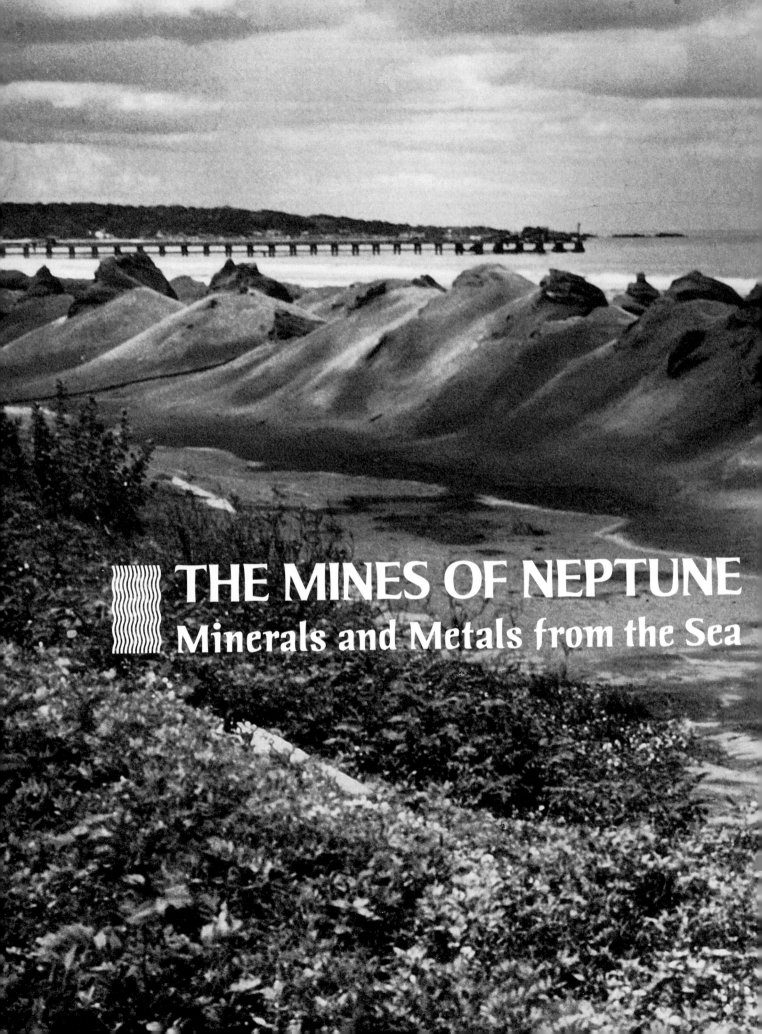

THE MINES OF NEPTUNE
Minerals and Metals from the Sea

By Elisabeth Mann Borgese
Foreword by Jan Tinbergen
Harry N. Abrams, Inc., Publishers, New York

Title page:
Mining of beach sand rich in heavy metals,
Sri Lanka.

Editor: Antony Dolman
Designer: Darilyn Lowe

Library of Congress Cataloging in Publication Data

Borgese, Elisabeth Mann.
The mines of Neptune.

Bibliography: p.
Includes index.
1. Ocean mining. 2. Mineral resources in submerged
lands. I. Title.
TN291.5.B67   1985   553′.09162   84-14451
ISBN 0-8109-1322-4

Printed and bound in Japan

⧙ Contents ⧙

▓ Foreword ▓

Today the world's oceans are used by humanity in many more ways than ever before. Not long ago, shipping and fishing were the only human activities connected with the huge water masses covering about three-quarters of the earth's surface; moreover, fishing possibilities seemed to have no limits. Now the character of both shipping and fishing has changed. Ships have become larger and larger. The increased use of oil requires ever-growing volumes to be transported by tankers, the dimensions of which have become next to unmanageable. Tanker accidents causing pollution of sea water and beaches sometimes assume disastrous proportions. Fishing, which actually is fish hunting, has also increased in volume with the use of "factory ships." An increasing number of fish species are threatened by overfishing. In areas where the depth of the sea is limited—the continental shelves—oil and natural gas can now be exploited by means of artificial islands.

On the bottom of the deep ("abyssal") seabed, large quantities of "nodules" can be found with a high content of nickel, copper, cobalt, manganese, and some other metals, which together constitute an enormous reserve.

The varied new possibilities of using—or abusing—the seas have necessitated the creation of a much more complicated Law of the Sea than the one that prevailed before. Compared with the period in which a simple principle could be the basis for agreement—the principle of *mare liberum*, the free use of

the seas—a much more complex set of rules is needed today, aiming at equity for all concerned. The interests now involved are many and different, including shipping, fishing, military uses, energy production, environmental protection, the interests of coastal nations—including big and small island states—and those of nations without any coastline. Since 1973, under the auspices of the United Nations, negotiations have been conducted regarding the new Law of the Sea. It has required a high level of sophistication and intellectual inventiveness to bring some harmony to this almost bewildering array of interests.

In 1967, when the first exchange of ideas on a new Law of the Sea began, a large part of the oceans had not been claimed by any nation as falling under its "sovereign rights." The great idea was launched that the unclaimed areas constituted a "common heritage of mankind," which might be the beginning of a supranational responsibility, requiring supranational rather than international law. In a world so much in need of a unified direction, this could prove to be the starting point.

Of course, coastal nations, one after the other, have tried to abuse this uncertain legal situation by claiming a zone of 200 nautical miles in which they would have exclusive economic sovereignty, whatever that might ultimately mean. But this still leaves a considerable portion of the oceans to some form of supranational decision-making, as embodied in the UN Convention on the Law of the

Sea, which was adopted on December 1, 1982 and has since been signed by 134 states.

A new technology is also required for the exploitation of the ocean's mineral wealth. This has already been developed by some enterprises in the industrialized countries. Without the Conference on the Law of the Sea, business as usual would prevail, and enterprises would start operations without being subject to any regulation. This would result in the appropriation of this additional resource, the seabed minerals, by the already prosperous countries. The new agency would change this course of events so that any such activity could be undertaken only as a joint venture with "the Enterprise," or in some other form of association with the Authority. This would mean that the proceeds derived from the mining of the nodules would have to be distributed between the licensing Authority and the licensee.

The subject of this book is the technology, ecology, and economy of ocean mining. The author, through her penetrating mind, and with the aid of her clear style and the impressive use of color photography, seeks to familiarize the reader, thought to be "the interested layman," with the technology now under development and so crucial to the redistributive processes which she and so many of us hope to see.

Elisabeth Mann Borgese has a special expertise when it comes to writing on ocean matters. She combines a thorough knowledge of the entire sequence of events since 1973 with a full devotion to the cause of the Third World. Her expertise made her a member of the Austrian delegation to the Conference on the Law of the Sea. She has witnessed at first hand each of the consecutive crises that have characterized the negotiating process and contributed to many of the sophisticated solutions found for the crises. Several of the new concepts which brought solutions were products of her creative mind.

Professor Mann Borgese has written extensively on the oceans, her writings covering more than three decades. *The Mines of Neptune* is the third in a trilogy of books in which she has summarized the ideas, insights, and knowledge accumulated over a distinguished career. The first of the trilogy was *The Drama of the Oceans,* published in 1976 and now translated into several languages. In it, she presented a comprehensive survey of all the issues and problems which will need to be confronted if the oceans are to be managed and conserved for the benefit of today's as well as future generations. It was a book that provided us with a broad panorama and which set the scene for more detailed treatments at a later date. Detailed treatment of fish farming followed in *Seafarm*, published in 1978. This fascinating book argued persuasively that the oceans, if properly managed, could be one of the keys to feeding the world's hungry population.

The Mines of Neptune provides us with detailed treatment of the mineral riches and resources of the oceans and the seabed. Like her other books, it challenges us to see how the proper use of these riches and resources could be instrumental in bringing about a fairer world. And like her other books, it blends a knowledge of the current attempts to find solutions to the "drama of the oceans" with ideas which transcend current notions of "political feasibility." I have little doubt that it will meet with the success it deserves.

Jan Tinbergen

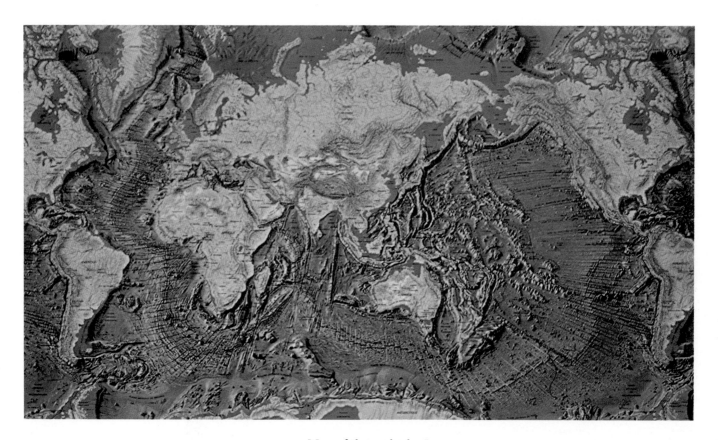

Map of the seabed.

Overleaf:
Sediment core: the green is silicates; the black
is sulphides; and the yellow and brown are limonites.

East Pacific Rise, 21°N.

East Pacific Rise.

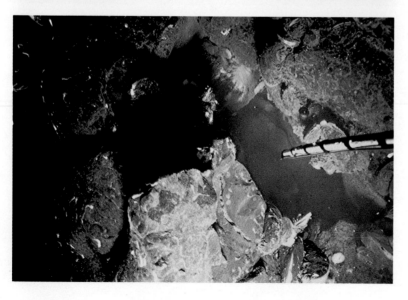

Active natural hot-air vent in
seafloor. Water temperature: up
to 13°C.

Left:
Bed of mussels with white brachyuran crabs, the Galapagos.

Below:
Bed of giant clams near a heat vent, taken in the Galapagos with the *Alvin* exterior camera.

Chain dredge partially filled with phosphorite nodules.

Opposite:
Beach placer of ilmenite (dark laminae),
Mozambique.

Survey catamaran identifying offshore
minerals in Sierra Leone.

∭ Introduction ∭
VULCAN AND NEPTUNE

Once upon a time there was an iron age, and a bronze age before that. Perhaps there was also a golden age, once upon a time.

Mythology associates various phases of human civilization with metals: with the character of the metals and the uses human beings made of them. So does anthropology.

The golden age, when human beings were as noble as the metal that gave it its name—human beings free from all hardship, and unaging—may belong to the realm of nostalgic imagination. But anthropologists agree that the first metal that humans chanced on and used for ornamental purposes was in fact gold.

Mythology traces human destiny down through a silver age whose inhabitants were inferior to those of the golden age. After silver came bronze, and generations of sturdy and violent men who in turn were to yield the earth to the iron race, the worst of all, an age in which men, treacherous and cruel, destroyed one another. The iron age marks the end of the human species. Beset by frightful symptoms of degeneracy (children were born with gray hair), the species was to be finally destroyed by Zeus.

Anthropology, too, places the bronze age before the iron age, the steel age of modern times. Our iron race, certainly, is treacherous and cruel, and the tokens of decay, due to the reckless tampering with our environment, are everywhere evident. It is all too possible that the ancients were right, and that our iron civilization will destroy itself.

Another civilization, however, may be rising from the ashes of the iron age. The World Tree that Zoroaster saw had many more branches than just gold, silver, bronze, and iron. We are seeing the future in riddles, and the mineral to characterize the coming generations of humans is not yet clearly discernible. It might be silicon, the mineral used to make the mysterious "chips," the basis of the awesome computer and microelectronics revolution that has begun to transform human society. The vast abyssal plain of the deep oceans are covered with silica, a compound of silicon and oxygen.

Silica formed, in fact, the oldest branch on the World Tree. It was the very first mineral ever mined by *Homo sapiens*. Deep in the stone age, man cut shafts through layers of solid chalk, and from the shafts he dug galleries supported by pillars, which followed the seams of silica chips, or flint, the basis of stone-age culture. In those times, just as in ours, the galleries occasionally caved in, burying the miners alive. Their remains have been unearthed in various European sites, with their tools—antler picks and bone shovels—in their skeleton hands. Thus the circle closes, and the cycle may be renewed. Who is to know?

What can be seen clearly, however, is the enormous importance of metals, metal mining, and metal processing in the history of civilization. Georgius Agricola, who wrote the first comprehensive mining treatise in 1556—a work astonishing in its modernity—put it as follows:

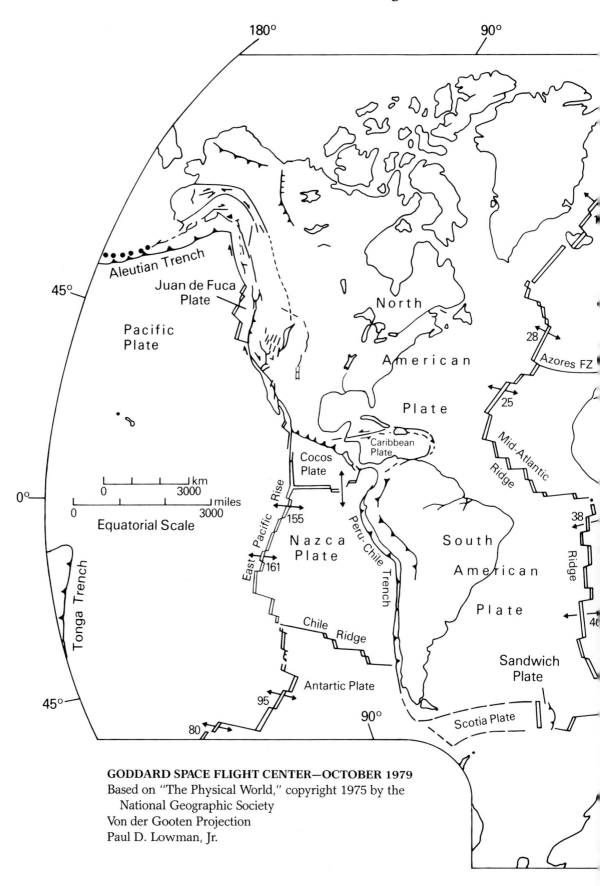

GODDARD SPACE FLIGHT CENTER—OCTOBER 1979
Based on "The Physical World," copyright 1975 by the
   National Geographic Society
Von der Gooten Projection
Paul D. Lowman, Jr.

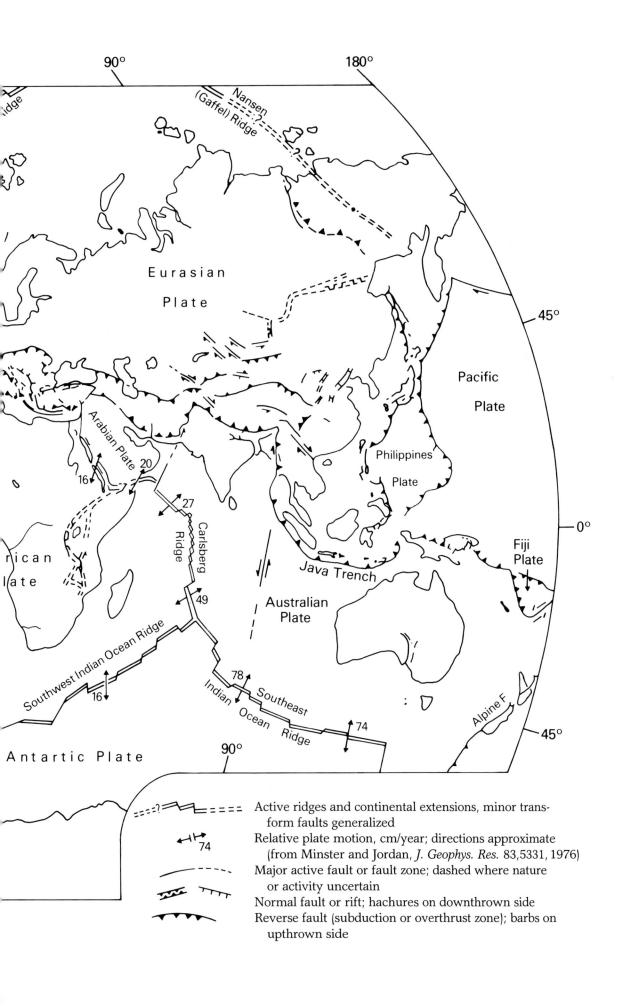

90°   180°

Nansen
(Gaffel) Ridge

Eurasian
Plate

45°

Pacific
Plate

Arabian Plate

20

16

Philippines

Plate

27

Carlsberg Ridge

0°

rican
late

49

Fiji
Plate

Java Trench

Australian
Plate

Southwest Indian Ocean Ridge

16

78

Southeast

Indian Ocean Ridge

74

Alpine F

45°

Antartic Plate   90°

=====?⌐⌐⌐=====   Active ridges and continental extensions, minor transform faults generalized

⊢⊣74   Relative plate motion, cm/year; directions approximate
(from Minster and Jordan, *J. Geophys. Res.* 83,5331, 1976)

‾‾‾‾ – – –   Major active fault or fault zone; dashed where nature
or activity uncertain

〰〰 ╥╥╥   Normal fault or rift; hachures on downthrown side

◤◤◤   Reverse fault (subduction or overthrust zone); barbs on
upthrown side

But what need of more words. If we remove metals from the service of men, all methods of protecting and sustaining health and more carefully preserving the course of life are done away with. If there were no metals, men would pass through a horrible and wretched existence in the midst of wild beasts; they would return to the acorns and fruits and berries of the forest. They would feed upon the herbs and roots which they plucked up with their nails. They would dig out caves in which to lie down at night, and by day they would rove in the woods and plains at random like beasts, and inasmuch as their condition is utterly unworthy of humanity, with its splendid and glorious natural endowment, will anyone be so foolish or so obstinate as not to allow that metals are necessary for food and clothing and that they tend to preserve life?

A second aspect that strikes one when looking at the history of civilizations through the history of mining is the totally earthbound, continental, mountainous character of mining. In Greek antiquity, miners were called "hill-men." This concept is also reflected in other languages. The German miner, for instance, is a *Bergman* (mountain man), and the medieval Bohemian miner was called *montanus*.

Metals were thought to grow, like living matter, in the mountains. Some peoples, the Malaysians for instance, believed that metals could flow through mountain veins toward a predetermined place if properly propitiated by a mining wizard. This Merlin of the mines could also make the metals move away if, for any reason, he was angry. That metals in the ground have souls was a belief shared by peoples in all parts of the world. Metals were associated with gnomes or demons or wights or dwarfs who inhabited the mountains where they plied their blacksmithing craft and commanded the immense treasures that issue from the bowels of the earth.

Hephaestos had his forge on Mount Olympus. Vulcan's workshop was on Mount Etna. It was an awesome place. Fire panted in the furnace, steel hissed in the caverns, and the Cyclopes processed the metal by mixing together rays of twisted hail, watery cloud, ruddy flame, and the winged southern wind. So earthbound was Vulcan's activity that his festival, the Vulcanalia, was marked by a strange ritual: the Roman patriarchs threw fish into his fire, offering creatures normally beyond the reach of this earthbound deity.

The immemorial association between metals and what was thought to be most earthy on earth is now being broken. Our *Weltanschauung*, our way of contemplating this world of ours, is changing, and as it does we no longer see ourselves as earthbound. Planet Earth is becoming Planet Ocean, and mining is moving into the deep seas—with ecological, economic, and social consequences we have barely begun to fathom.

Before trying to describe this transformation it may be worthwhile to indicate some of the curious parallels between the miner and the mariner. This may help us understand and anticipate the amazing amalgamation of the law of the sea and mining law which is being attempted by our generation.

In classical antiquity—both Greek and Roman—the fate of the oarsman and that of the miner were about the worst that could befall a wretched human being, whether a prisoner of war or a delinquent sold into the hardest of slaveries. The life of the galley slave, as documented in ancient texts, has been depicted in many modern novels and films. Suffice it to recall Ben Hur, chained to his bench in filth and stench, wracked by hunger and thirst and whipped almost to unconsciousness. When he could take no more and died, the galley slave was unceremoniously thrown overboard. There were galley slaves throughout the Middle Ages, even into modern times. In the Baltic the use of galleys lingered into the nineteenth century.

The mines were similarly manned by slaves. Among the Greeks and Romans, condemnation to the mines, *damnatio ad metalla*, was considered a more terrible punishment than being sent to the galleys or to the arena to fight the lions. Only the death penalty was considered worse. The same was true in Egypt. In *De lapidibus,* written about 300 B.C., Theophrastus describes the miners' lot as follows: "Those who dig in the mines cannot stand upright at their work but are obliged to lie down either on their backs or on one side." Diodorus recounts how "many of them die by reason of excessive ill treatment, for relaxation or rest from their labors is not allowed; but for the blows of their masters compelling them to endure their dreadful misfortunes, they miserably abandon their life." Mine slavery, like galley slavery, survived far into the modern era. It was widespread throughout the eighteenth century and in some parts of the world even existed into the nineteenth century.

The status of the miner has, however, undergone a significant change. As the demand for metals increased and more highly developed skills became associated with the exploration and exploitation of mines, the job had to be upgraded. The miners gradually developed into a special class with special rights and privileges. They were, for example, exempt from military service, and they had standing before special courts. They even developed a special kind of democracy, "a state within a state," as T. A. Rickard points out in his mining history, *Man and Metal.*

Parallels could be drawn between this development and the development of the very special rights and duties of the mariner, from classical Rhodian Sea Law through the Laws of Oléron. Under the hardship conditions of life at sea, and with the development of special skills, a special kind of "democracy" evolved, with its own laws. Thus, one law had it that the captain could not determine alone whether weather conditions were going to be favorable enough to permit the undertaking of a journey. This meteorological question had to be decided by a vote of the crew!

At the same time something developed that was called "the freedom of the miner,"

or "mining freedom," or *Bergbaufreiheit,* as it was called in late medieval Germany. Any person had the right to prospect for metal, wherever it might be found, and to stake a claim. The parallel with the "freedom of the sea" is obvious. Under this freedom, the miner, like the mariner, became pioneer, explorer, and frontiersman. Sovereignty, limiting the freedom of the seas, went as far as a cannon could shoot. The length of a miner's claim was the distance he could throw his axe!

The mine, like the sea, is three-dimensional, raising issues of conflicting rights and regimes. Does the owner of the surface land also own the underlying minerals? According to some, the ancient Romans for instance, he does: his rights extend "down to the boundaries of hell." According to others, for instance the Germans in the Middle Ages, he does not. Frederick Barbarossa laid down the law that surface tenure and mineral ownership were separate matters, and while the surface could be subject to private ownership, the sovereign was the sole proprietor of all mines.

Similarly, there are conflicting theories about the status of the surface and water column of the ocean on the one hand and the subjacent ocean floor on the other. Traditionally there was only one regime for ocean space beyond the narrow limits of the territorial sea, and that was the freedom of the sea. Nobody cared about the ocean floor. It was very un-real estate. As it was explored, however, the conflicting theories emerged. There were those who held that the ocean floor was covered by the principle of the freedom of the seas. Others upheld the view that the freedom of the seas could not apply and that the ocean floor and its mineral resources were governed by another principle: that of the common heritage of mankind, where mankind as a whole is substituted for the sovereign. Contemporary sea law accepts the principle of two different regimes: one for the waters of the sea and the other for the underlying ocean floor with its minerals and metals.

Greek mythology has it that the goddess Hera, disgusted with her deformed son Hephaestos, hurled him from heaven, and he landed in the sea. There he is said to have been rescued by the sea goddesses Eurynome and Thetis, and to have dwelt in the oceans for nine years.

It took mankind a couple of thousand years to discover that Hephaestos, the god of fire and metallurgy, must have left many of his elements strewn about the ocean floor; to discover that he must have built his smithies in huge volcanoes along vast mountain ranges, calling forth metals and minerals from the true depths of the earth. When he renounced the oceans and took to his earthbound mountainous workshop, he left his mines to Poseidon, or Neptune.

Our discovery of the mines of Neptune has totally revolutionized our concept of the earth and its history. What once appeared so stable has now become all motion, as oceans and continents are seen to be created and re-created in a continuous process, recycling their elements.

Cycles have no beginning and no end: we may enter the cyclic process at any point. Let us join the cycle at the middle of the floor of the deep ocean. There we find a mountain range, only discovered in the 1950s and 1960s, that is unlike any with which we are familiar (Figure 1). "Millions of square miles of a tangled jumble of massive peaks, saw-toothed ridges, earthquake-shattered cliffs, valleys, lava formations of every conceivable shape—that is the mid-Ocean ridge." That is how one of its discoverers, the late Dr. Maurice Ewing of the Lamont-Doherty Geological Observatory, described a mountain range, much bigger than any on earth, that runs through the whole ocean system for more than 110,000 kilometers.

The ridge is cleft lengthwise by a deep rift, or valley, from which molten basalt pours forth. The basalt builds the mountains, adding to the ocean floor and forcing it apart. The ocean floor appears to grow a few centimeters per year, about as much as a child

may grow during the same period. During a human lifetime, the sea floor moves about the length of a human body, admittedly a lamentably anthropocentric way of looking at these mountainous processes.

The continents, made of granitic rock which is lighter than the oceanic basalt, slide on huge "tectonic plates" on the basaltic ground. They separate where the sea floor spreads and the ocean grows. The Atlantic is a young and growing ocean. So are the Red Sea and the Gulf of Mexico.

There are deep trenches along the rims of the continents which devour the spreading ocean floor. The earth quakes, and its molten core spills over the brim of volcanoes all along mountain arcs that border the deep trenches. When the ocean floor is consumed by these marginal trenches faster than it is produced at the center, the ocean shrinks, eventually to disappear. When continents clash over a disappearing ocean, mountains pile up, pushing submarine surfaces high into the sky. The Mediterranean and the Pacific are shrinking oceans.

Thus the earth is remade, inside out and outside in, about once every 300 or 400 million years. As continents drift and turn and gyrate, the earth's magnetic poles wander, and climates, flora, and fauna are in constant transformation.

Sea water, covering over 70 percent of the earth's surface, interacts with the atmosphere and acts on the world's climate. Warmed on the sun-lit surface, and cooler down in the dark deep, sea water also interacts with the oceanic crust. Cold sea water has percolated into the crust through cracks and crevices for millions of years and slowly reacted with the rocks in the crust. This happens at the bottom of the sea, just as it happens with rainwater and terrestrial rock. Rainwater sometimes seeps some 30 to 50 kilometers into the ground and returns to the surface as thermal springs.

As it is heated by volcanic rock, the sea water absorbs heavy metals. The hot brine, with its heavy-metal content, eventually returns to the ocean floor. There it mixes with

Table 1: Classification of Marine Mineral Resources

DISSOLVED	UNCONSOLIDATED			CONSOLIDATED
	Continental Shelf (0–200 m)	Continental Slope (200–3,500 m)	Deep Sea‡ (3,500–6,000 M)	

SEA WATER:
  Fresh water*
  Metals and salts
  of:
    Magnesium*
    Sodium*
    Calcium*
    Bromine*
    Potassium
    Sulfur
    Strontium
    Boron
    Uranium†
    Other elements
METALLIFEROUS
BRINES:‡
  Concentrations of:
    Zinc
    Copper
    Lead
    Silver
	NONMETALLICS:
	  Sand and gravel†
	  Lime sands and
	    shells†
	  Silica sand†
	  Semiprecious
	    stones†
	  Industrial sands†
	  Phosphorite
	  Aragonite
	  Barite*
	  Glauconite
	HEAVY MINERALS:
	  Magnetite†
	  Hmenite†
	  Rutile†
	  Monazite†
	  Chromite
	  Zircon†
	  Cassiterite*
	RARE AND PRECIOUS MINERALS:
	  Diamonds*
	  Platinum
	  Gold†
	  Native copper
		AUTHIGENICS:
		  Phosphorite‡
		  Ferromanganese ox-
		    ides and associated
		    minerals
		  Metalliferous mud
		    with:
		    Zinc
		    Copper
		    Lead
		    Silver
			AUTHIGENICS:
			  Ferromanganese nod-
			    ules and associated
			    Cobalt
			    Nickel
			    Copper
			SEDIMENTS
			  Red clays
			  Calcareous ooze
			  Siliceous ooze
				DISSEMINATED,
				MASSIVE VEIN,
				TABULAR, OR
				STRATIFIED DE-
				POSITS OF:
				  Coal
				  Ironstone
				  Limestone
				  Sulfur
				  Tin
				  Gold
				  Metallic sulfides
				  Metallic salts
				  Hydrocarbons

SOURCE: M. J. Cruickchank, *Marine Mining. SME Mining Engineering Handbook*, 1973, section 20.
* Currently recovered commercially offshore
† Recovered in coastal areas: may include some offshore activity
‡ Under research and development

the colder bottom water and the metals are precipitated and sedimented. Basins with rich sediments of this kind have been discovered in the middle of the Red Sea. They are likely to be found in areas of similar geophysical conformation, such as the Gulf of California, or along the mid-oceanic ridges in general.

"In this case," Dr. B. D. Lonkarevic of the Bedford Institute of Oceanography has speculated, such deposits "might occur anywhere along the 70,000 km long chain of mid-ocean mountains. If this is the case, the amount of metals available to the miners of the future is truly staggering. Simply beyond comprehension. Even speculation about the exploitation of this resource would sound like science fiction today."

Metals and minerals can be found on the continental shelves, on the continental slopes, and on the deep seabed (Table 1, Figure 2). They reach the oceans from the interior of the earth and through run-offs from land. Rivers carry eroded mountain substances into the sea. Metals and minerals reach the oceans from the atmosphere in the

2. Schematic cross-section through continental margin and adjoining deep sea, showing mineral potentials

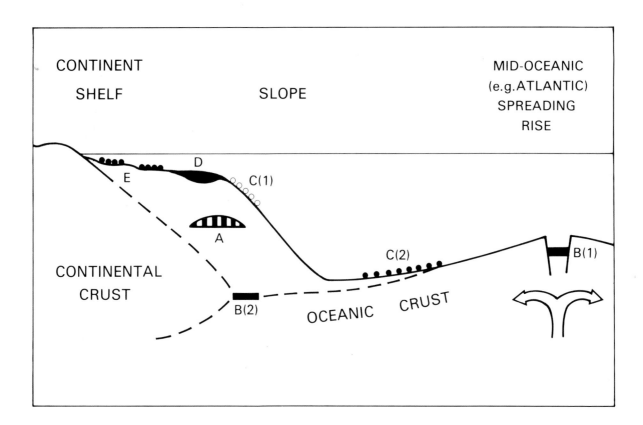

(A-Hydrocarbon deposits; B-Hydrothermal (metalliferous) mud: B(1)-recent, B(2)-older lithified deposits; C(1)-phosphorites, C(2)-manganese nodules; D-metalliferous ooze; E-placers).

form of heavy-metal pollution. They fall from outer space: about 8 to 10 tons of meteoric iron, nickel, and silicon arrive each year from outer space and settle in red clay sediments on the abyssal plain of the deep ocean. Aluminum oxide, manganese, cobalt, copper, nickel, and vanadium are other components of this red clay, which covers half the floor of the Pacific Ocean and about one-fourth of the Atlantic and Indian Ocean seabed, at an average depth of 3 km. And right along the middle, in a band about 125 km across and 1600 km long, running roughly east–west along the southern edge of the equatorial belt at a depth of about 1,500 to 5,000 meters—in the Pacific, Atlantic, and Indian oceans—there is an enormous field of polymetallic nodules. There are literally trillions of them, ranging in size from golf balls to large potatoes, glistening black and porous. They contain billions of dollars' worth of nickel, copper, cobalt, magnesium, iron, and a number of other metals (Table 2).

The abyssal plain, with its sediments of clays and biogenic oozes formed from the calcareous remains of trillions of tiny animals—the radiolarians—is the biggest plain on earth. It is not a smooth plain, however. Sea mounds, submerged peaks of 1,000 meters' altitude, are strewn throughout the plain. On the seaward side, the plain is bordered by a hilly region, the so-called abyssal hills province, the promontory of the mid-ocean ridge. On the landward side, the plain gives way to the gently sloping continental rise.

On the continental margins and shelves, metals have been discovered, and mined, all over the world—chromite and platinum, gold and silver, lead and copper, tin and iron ore.

Offshore salt domes yield vast quantities of sulphur. Salt domes are also often associated with the presence of oil, although no one as yet knows how far out or how deep down. Such domes, steeply rising structures that distort the sediment layers above them and thus form cavities in which oil is trapped, have been found under 3,500 meters of water and 5,000 meters of sediment.

Recent studies suggest that the potential of as yet unexplored deep oceans could conceivably double present estimated world oil resources.

"Sea coal" was mined in England in the thirteenth century. "As the tide cometh in it bringeth a small wash of sea coal which is employed to the making of salt and the fuel of the poor fisher towns adjoining," a sixteenth-century chronicle records. The monks of Newcastle Abbey obtained a grant from their landlord as early as 1235 to build a road to the shore for the convevance of seaweed, *alga maris,* and sea coal, *carbo maris.* The records show that coal was not only gathered from the beaches but also excavated from trenches and tunnels. There was a tax on the digging of sea coal, which apparently caused environmental problems at a very early date. In 1306 Parliament petitioned King Edward I to prohibit the use of sea coal in London on account of its "sulferous smoke and savor of the firing."

Sea coal mines are tunneled from land and dug from islands or platforms. There are well over a hundred mines in operation today; some reach a depth of 2,200 meters under 110 meters of water and are up to 8 kilometers from shore.

That the ocean water itself, moving over the sea floor and continental shelves, contains vast masses of dissolved metals was known to Aristotle. Georgius Agricola had the following comment in his treatise on mining:

> *Springs may discharge their waters into the sea, a lake, a marsh or a stream, but the sand of the seashore is rarely washed, for although the water flowing down from the springs into the sea carries some metals or gems with it, yet these substances can scarcely ever be reclaimed because they are dispersed through the immense body of the waters and mixed up with other sands and scattered far and wide in different directions, or they sink down into the depth of the sea.*

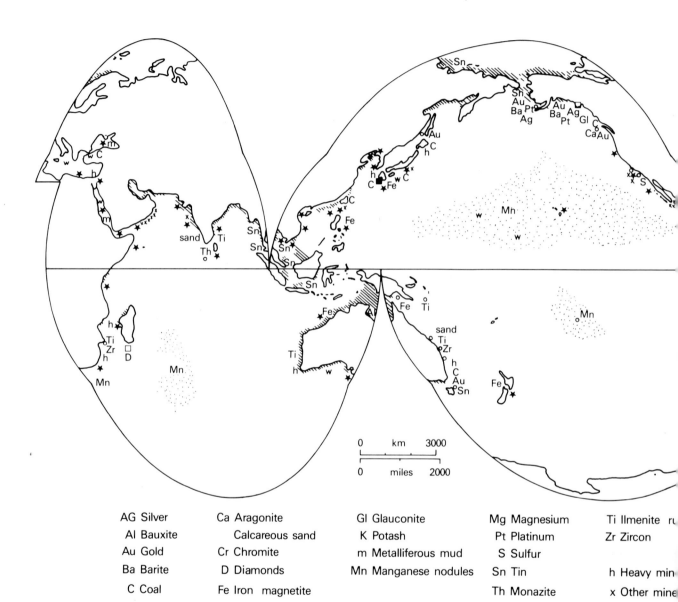

AG Silver	Ca Aragonite	Gl Glauconite	Mg Magnesium	Ti Ilmenite ru
Al Bauxite	Calcareous sand	K Potash	Pt Platinum	Zr Zircon
Au Gold	Cr Chromite	m Metalliferous mud	S Sulfur	
Ba Barite	D Diamonds	Mn Manganese nodules	Sn Tin	h Heavy min
C Coal	Fe Iron magnetite		Th Monazite	x Other mine

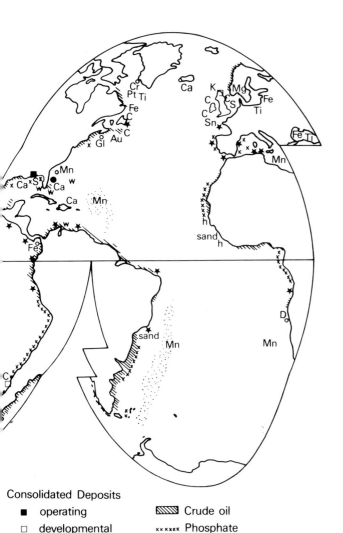

Consolidated Deposits

- ■ operating
- □ developmental

Unconsolidated Deposits

- ● operating
- ○ developmental

- ▨ Crude oil
- xxxxx Phosphate
- ★ Salt
- W Fresh water

Modern science corroborates the insight of the ancient scholar. Ocean water is a gigantic liquid mine containing at least sixty useful minerals and metals in stunning quantities, such as 10 million tons of gold, over 15 billion tons of manganese, and probably over 20 billion tons of uranium. The total mass of dissolved material has been estimated at over 15 quadrillion tons (see Table 8).

The extraction of these treasures has been the dream of many a metallurgist. Dr. Fritz Haber, Nobel Prize–winning German chemist, spent a number of years in efforts to encourage the ocean to yield its gold—or a modest portion of it. Guided by patriotic considerations, he suggested that the potential rewards would make it possible for Germany to pay the reparations due to the victorious allies after the First World War. The German research ship *Meteor,* in one of the more important oceanographic expeditions made during the early part of this century, cruised the oceans for two years (1925–27), probing metal contents and testing extraction methods, especially between South Africa and South America.

The gold was there, but it was so diffused (0.008 mg per ton of sea water) that the cost of the energy required to extract it was far higher than the price it would command. Sea gold clearly did not offer an economical way to pay the reparations. "There is nothing more complex and varied than the ocean environment," Haber concluded. "Possible, that some time somewhere a site may be identified where precious metals accumulate with some regularity. Possible also, that such a site is located in accessible climatic conditions and that such circumstance may rekindle once more the thought of processing gold from seawater. I have given up looking for this needle in a haystack."

Other metals and minerals were more readily accessible and have been extracted in increasing quantities. Thirty percent of the world's production of common salt, for instance, is extracted from sea water (sea salt) by a process that is as simple as it is ancient. Sea water is trapped in shallow ponds along

Table 2: Reserves of Metals in Polymetallic Nodules of the Pacific Ocean

Element	Amount of Element in Nodules (Billions of Tons)*	Reserves in Nodules at Consumption Rate of 1960 (Years)†	Approximate World Land Reserves of Elements (Years)‡	Reserves in Nodules/ Reserves on Land	U.S. Rate of Consumption of Element in 1960 (Millions of Tons per Year)§	Rates of Accumulation of Element in Nodules (Millions of Tons per Year)	Rate of Accumulation/ Rate of U.S. Consumption	World Consumption/ U.S. Consumption
Magnesium	25	600,000	L¶	...	.04	.18	4.5	2.5
Aluminum	43	20,000	100	200	2.0	.30	.15	2.0
Titanium	9.9	2,000,000	L¶	...	.30	.069	.23	4.0
Vanadium	.8	400,000	L¶	...	.002	.0056	2.8	4.0
Manganese	358	400,000	100	4,000	.8	2.5	3.0	8.0
Iron	207	2,000	500#	4	100	1.4	4.01	2.5
Cobalt	5.2	200,000	40	5,000	.008	.036	4.5	2.0
Nickel	14.7	150,000	100	1,500	.11	.102	1.0	3.0
Copper	7.9	6,000	40	150	1.2	.055	.05	4.0
Zinc	.7	1,000	100	10	.9	.0048	.005	3.5
Gallium	.015	150,000	...	...	.0001	.0001	1.0	...
Zirconium	.93	+100,000	+100	1,000	.0013	.0065	5.0	...
Molybdenum	.77	30,000	500	60	.25	.0054	.2	2.0
Silver	.001	100	100	1	.006	.00003	.005	...
Lead	1.3	1,000	40	50	1.0	.009	.009	2.5

SOURCE: John Mero, *The Marine Resources of the Sea*, p. 196.
* All tonnages in metric units
† Amount available in the nodules divided by the consumption rate
‡ Calculated as the element in metric tons (from U.S. Bureau of Mines Bulletin no. 556)
§ Calculated as the element in metric tons
¶ Present reserves so large as to be essentially unlimited at present rates of consumption
# Including deposits of iron that are at present considered marginal

4. Marine mineral resources and development

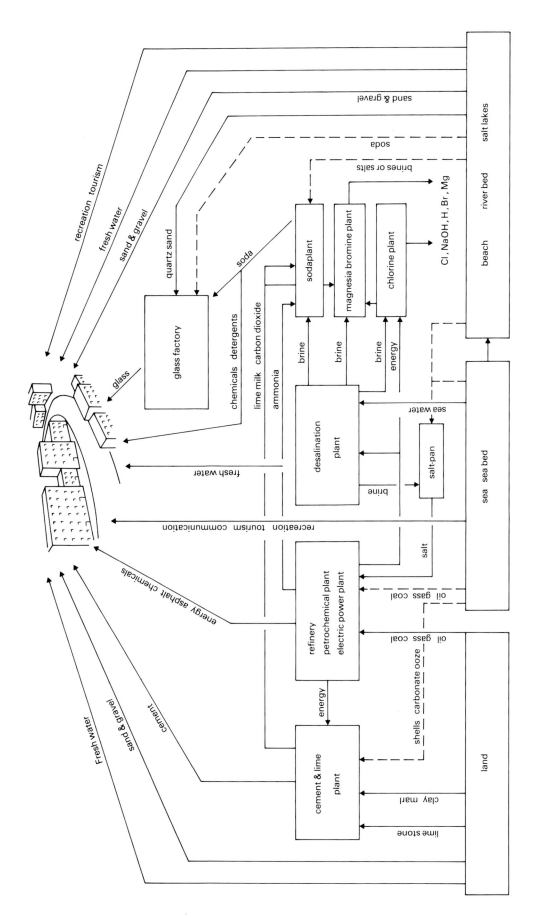

the coast, the water is allowed to evaporate in the sun's heat, and the salt remains behind, encrusting the bottom and sides of the pools.

Seventy percent of the total world production of bromine and 60 percent of magnesium are extracted from the seas, often together with sodium chloride, or common salt.

High energy costs were one of the reasons why the dreams of scientists like Dr. Haber were frustrated. Even if the energy could have been found, the environmental problems caused by the excessive use of energy (thermopollution) might have turned dreams of gold into an ecological nightmare. But what was impossible or dangerous in the past may well soon be feasible and safe through bioindustrial processes. Through such processes we may not even have to do the job ourselves: we can use animals and plants to do the work for us. Certain sea worms, the ascidian for instance, concentrate vanadium in their bodies. Lobsters extract copper from sea water. Many sea animals and plants concentrate heavy metals. Genetic engineering may increase this capacity. Algologists are presently working, in the USA and USSR, on experimental "uranium farms," where uranium is concentrated by algae and extracted from them with a side product of methane and fertilizer.

There may be other possibilities. Imagine the discovery of rays which could illuminate the mines of Neptune: rays that made the dissolved metals and minerals glitter in the dark waters like myriad tiny stars; that enabled metal veins to glisten in the bedrock and glow through the sediments, cobalt blue and copper red, silver and gold; that made diamonds sparkle, and turned glauconite greensands lucent, like a sea of emeralds!

No one, not even in the most daring fairy tales, has ever seen the oceans in this light. No one ever has seen the mines of Neptune. A glimmer, however, has entered the inner eye of modern industrial civilization. The industrial revolution is penetrating deeper and deeper into the oceans, and mining, the most earthbound of all earthly industries, sciences, and traditions, is becoming a marine industry—partially at first, very likely totally at a later stage (Table 3).

Why this should be happening defies any simple explanation. Human beings are inquisitive and expansive by nature. As science opens vistas of new realms in outer space and other planets, in the inner reaches of the atom, on the bottom of the seas, in the dark recesses of the past, and the mysteries of the human mind, so technology follows and forges new tools. What humans *can* do they *will* do, if only because they *can*. Like climbing the highest mountain from the most rugged side.

The inquisitiveness of the human soul, however, is not enough to explain the transformation of a vast economic—or more than that, anthropological—system. A few medallions struck from the metals that have lain at the bottom of the oceans for hundreds of millions of years might be sufficient to satisfy such inquisitiveness. But human beings are not only inquisitive. They are also greedy, obsessed with miserly instincts. Enough is never enough; there must always be more. Futurologists of recent decades have made a science of predicting that "nonrenewable resources" are fast running out. No wonder people are happy to discover that there may be more than twice as much of these resources in the oceans than there ever were on earth.

More careful analysis, however, reveals that the metals and minerals which we are beginning to mine from the seas are still quite abundant on land. Nickel, copper, cobalt, and manganese, the object of nodule mining, are still plentiful on terra firma, and can be extracted without the huge investments and the transformation of the international order which marine mining entails. To see this, it is enough to compare tables of land-based reserves and resources of these metals with the estimated world demand up to the year 2000. The United States Office of Ocean Resources and Scientific Policy Coordination has provided us with just such a table (Table 4). Looking at the table, we can

Table 3: Ongoing and Possible Future Marine Mining of Unconsolidated Surficial Deposits

Commodity	Ore Mineral	Grade of Ore*	Price Range (US$)†
NONMETALLIC:			
Silica	Quartz sand	76.93	29–92/st
Lime	Shells and shell sands	1,428.6	1.40/st‡
Magnesite	Magnesite	33.33	60–100/st
Sand and gravel	Various	1,923.1	1.04–7.87/st
Phosphate	Phosphorite nodules and sand	307.7	6.50–1.02
Topaz	Topaz	1 ct/yd^3	1–5/ct
Spinel	Spinel	.2 ct/yd^3	5–100/ct
Corundum	Corundum	28.55	70–130/st
HEAVY MINERAL SANDS:			
Beryllium	Beryl	66.67	30–35/st
Titanium	Rutile	11.43	175/st
	Ilmenite	101.8	22–24/lt
Chromium	Chromite	93.33	24–56/lt
Zirconium	Zircon	40.0	56–70/lt
Manganese	Hausmannite, braunite	36.72	61–68/lt
Iron	Magnetite	203.64	11/lt
Thorium	Monazite	12.44	180–200/lt
Columbium	Columbite (10:1)	1.25	1,600–1,700/st
Rare earths	Group of 15 Me oxides	7.15	.14–3.00/lb§
Tin	Cassiterite	.7463	2.80/st¶
Mercury	Cinnabar	.498	125.5/fl(76 lb)
PRECIOUS AND RARE METALS:			
Diamonds	Diamond (industrial)	.25 ct/yd^3	4–50/ct
Copper	Native metal	2.04	.49–.53/lb
Silver	Native metal	.6369 oz/yd^3	1.57/oz
Gold	Native metal	.0203 tr oz/yd^3	49.26–49.46/tr oz
PLATINUM GROUP	Native metal	.0091 tr oz/yd^3	110/tr oz
DEEP-SEA AUTHIGENES:			
Mn/Fe/Co/Ni/Cu	Manganese nodules	66.84	29.92–56.61/st#
Au/Ag/Cu/Pb/Zn	Metalliferous oozes	481.93	4.15–12/st**

SOURCE: G. J. S. Govett and M. H. Govett, *World Mineral Supplies.*

Note: st = short ton, lt = long ton, ct = carat, fl = fluid, tr oz = troy ounce

* Pound per yd^3 unless otherwise specified (to convert to kg/m^3 multiply by 0.342)

† Low value in price range used; prices from *Engineering and Mining Journal* (May 1972) and U.S. Bureau of Mines, *Minerals Yearbook, 1970* (Washington, D.C.: U.S. Bureau of Mines, 1970)

‡ Calculated from per-ton value of calcium in shell at 40 percent of this value, from atomic weights

§ Using $1.50 as the average value, rather than the low price in the price range

¶ Calculated from per-pound value (1972) of tin at 79 percent market value, from atomic weight

Varies from average Atlantic to highest Pacific; data from Mero, *The Mineral Resources of the Sea*

** As above, wet value

see that the pressure on resources is at present insufficient to bring about the transformation, although in the long term marine resources will have to be utilized in order to supplement decreasing land resources.

But there must be other factors accelerating the shift from land-based to marine resources at this time. Prices, certainly, will be highly influential. If sea mining becomes cheaper than land mining, the world will go sea mining. That is as certain as a law of nature.

Prices, of course, are themselves the result of complex processes. Fuel prices will have a significant impact on the cost both of transportation and of processing metals and minerals from the sea. As technologies become available to utilize renewable energy from the oceans themselves, rather than having to depend on spiraling oil prices, ocean mining will become more economical.

Technology as a whole, obviously, is a crucial factor. And here an interesting devel-

Table 4: Adequacy of World Reserves and Resources of Metals to Meet Cumulative Demand up to Year 2000

	RATIO OF RESERVES TO CUMULATIVE DEMAND UP TO YEAR 2000			RATIO OF RESOURCES (OTHER THAN RESERVES) TO CUMULATIVE DEMAND UP TO YEAR 2000		
	Low	**Medium**	**High**	**Low**	**Medium**	**High**
Nickel	230%	204%	152%	438%	388%	359%
Copper	173%	146%	126%	434%	368%	318%
Cobalt	144%	122%	107%	268%	223%	200%
Manganese	183%	173%	150%	532%	503%	436%

Note: "Reserves" here means "proven reserves"; "resources" is used in a more comprehensive sense, indicating unexplored resources, existing on circumstantial evidence.
SOURCE: U. S. Department of Commerce, Office of Ocean Resources and Scientific Policy Coordination, *Cobalt, Copper, Nickel and Manganese: Future Supply and Demand Implications for Deep Seabed Mining.*

ture. While it is not likely that the cost of sea mining will decrease as sensationally as, for instance, the cost of microelectronics, it is nevertheless likely that it will go down as new generations of mining technology are developed. John Mero, a pioneer of seabed mining, has predicted that, compared with mining on land, where $9 of capital may produce $1 a year, $1 of capital will return at least $3 from ocean mining. Although opinions differ as to the time frame and the magnitude of price reduction, there is general agreement that seabed mining will reduce prices of minerals and metals and that it will be economical.

opment can be observed. During its first stage, deep-sea mining is a gradual extension of shallow-water mining. Longer and longer cables and shafts reaching deeper and deeper down, increasingly more complex remote controls—but no matter how deep, gathering and lifting is done *from the surface* of the water, whether from ships or platforms and rigs. This method of seafloor mining has been compared to the harvesting of a field of potatoes from a plane flying at an altitude of 5,000 meters, by night and while the sky is cloudy and the field wrapped in dense fog! As long as this method prevails, cost rises in proportion to depth.

Then comes a conceptual breakthrough, one already being pioneered by some scientists, especially in Germany and Japan. The mining part—the gathering of the nodules—will be done *at the bottom of the sea,* no longer from the water surface. It will be done by self-propelled unmanned vehicles, supervised, perhaps, by bathyscaphs. It will be carried out by tractorlike "moon buggies," able to move without hazard over the unevennesses of the ocean floor, eliminating the need for the long cables which, confronted with the same unevennesses, will not only be subjected to stresses and strains but may even break. When the nodules are conveniently arranged by the deep-sea mining buggies, they will be sucked up by vacuum-cleaner-like stationary gear. Once this conceptual barrier is breached, then, as John Craven, another of the pioneers in deep-sea technology has put it, "Deeper is cheaper."

Related to the price factor, but beset with a number of other social implications, is the factor of labor. Land mining is labor-intensive, and with rising costs of labor the cost of mining increases. Land mining, furthermore, is a hardship job. There may no longer be mine slaves, but sickness and tragedy still disfigure the industry: the black lungs of the coal miners in Pennsylvania, the limbs of natives torn apart by mine explosions in postcolonial Africa, the unnumbered deaths by drowning or asphyxiation, often avoidable if safety measures were applied and respected, all still exist—the bequest of a social, economic, and technological order that is (and must be) on its way out.

Ocean mining technology is highly capital-intensive and mechanized, not labor-intensive. The scientist-worker of the ocean mining future will know his own hazards and thrills; but there will be few of these workers, not masses impelled by poverty to endure routinized hardship, institutionalized peril. In this, seabed mining technology belongs to a wider complex of sophisticated new technologies, a complex that includes space and satellite technologies, electronic and computer technologies, and biological and chemical technologies. These technologies have revolutionized the science of warfare and are transforming production processes and industrial systems, worker/employer relations, and the relations between industrialized and nonindustrialized countries. These technologies are upon us. They cannot be disinvented. They *will* be used because they *can* be used. How they will be used, and whether it will be possible to cushion their unsettling social and international side effects, is up to us.

Furthermore, there may be a strong environmental factor that helps hasten the shift from land mining to ocean mining. Land mining sites may compete with sites for agricultural use, grazing, or human habitation. Or they may just despoil nature, or what is left of it. This is an argument Agricola attempted to resolve four hundred years ago; it is much harder to resolve in our crowded world of today. One modern way of dealing with polluting or hazardous industries is to move them out to sea, onto artificial islands remote from the centers of human habitation. The same goes for mining. There is more space out there—the farther out, the better—and there is less competition between uses and between users. Certainly, seabed mining must not interfere with shipping routes; cables must not be damaged by seafloor dredging; conflicts must be avoided between military uses (the installation of listening devices, the use of antisubmarine warfare technology) and seabed mining. Fisheries must not be unduly disturbed. It would indeed be perverse—and this is the other side of the environmental coin—if, having wrecked the earth, mankind were now to proceed unscrupulously to destroy the ocean environment from which all life originated and on which it still largely depends.

Prudence is all the more indicated since we still know so very little about the flora and fauna of the deep ocean beds. Sponges, fans, feathers, and anemones grow in the abysses, coelenterates and stalked sea pens. Many of the creatures of the dark deep seas are brightly luminescent, glowing in the abyssal night. Sea lilies, starfish, urchins, and cucumbers inhabit all latitudes and depths. Feather gardens, mosses, and meadows become denser closer to shore.

It is still a generally held assumption, however, that life in the deep oceans is scarce. According to some estimates, the mid-ocean abyssal plain is inhabited by barely a milligram of living matter per square meter, compared to 200 grams on the outer continental shelf, and 5,000 grams in the teeming inshore waters. But who knows? New discoveries constantly alter the picture.

A recent expedition, in the context of the Rivera Submersible Experiments (RISE) Program, directed its vessels to the axis of the East Pacific Rise, between Baja California and the Mazatlán coast of Mexico, 20°–24° north and 106°–110° west. The purpose was to study the creation of new crust, crustal motion, metallogenesis, hydrothermal effects, and unexplored types of benthic biological communities. The main work was carried out on the East Pacific Rise crest at 21° north, where the Pacific and the Rivera plates are separating at the rapid rate of 6 centimeters a year. There, 2,400 meters down, hydrothermal vents were discovered. They emit water, from fissures and hairline cracks in the fresh pillow lava, at temperatures of 23°C, which quickly mixes with the surrounding cold bottom waters (2°C). In some places, water jets, spouting at high velocity from sulphite-blackened "chimneys," were found to have temperatures of over 350°C.

These warm water oases in the deep cold desert were found to be teeming with life: a flourishing crab population, and large white clams, some reaching a length of 25 centimeters. The surface of the lava pillows was encrusted with white-tubed serpulid polychaetes. There were small, light-colored eellike fishes and various kinds of limpets. The most surprising find was giant tube worms, clustering around the warm water vents. Two to 3 centimeters in diameter, they reached a length of up to 3 meters and wore red, gill-like crowns. They are the largest worms ever found. Deep down in the darkness, creatures grow larger than in the sunlit surface of the waters. Their growth is not based on photosynthesis, as in our world, but occurs on the basis of chemical transformations (chemosynthesis) effected by bacteria, the basic foodstuff of the animals in that other world.

How many such "oases" exist on the deep ocean floor is not known, nor is it known whether the fauna associated with the East Pacific Rise—or the Galapagos Rift, where Expedition FAMOUS made similar discoveries—is universally distributed, or whether the type of life varies geographically.

The *SEDCO* is a magnificent ship, originally designed for oil drilling but recently re-equipped for nodule gathering and lifting. A film was made during its recent, highly successful mining tests in the Mid Pacific. To watch the film is to observe both the past and the future. You see photographic equipment sinking down through 5 kilometers of water. When its floodlights hit the abyssal plain, the cameras start shooting pictures. They show strange tracks on the smooth red clay surface, winding in loops and curves—eerily clear in the fully lit zone, losing themselves in the dark. Who knows whence they came or where they are going? Looking like a script telling us something about the origin of life in the oceans, and perhaps about its future, the tracks may also tell us something about *our* origin and *our* future. No one has ever seen such writing, not since a hand appeared and wrote in letters unknown upon the wall of King Belsazar's Babylonian palace: "*Mene:* Counted and measured has God the realm of the deep seabed. *Tekel:* Weighted and found wanting, our efforts thus far to manage this common heritage of mankind more successfully, more prudently and more equitably by establishing a new order for ocean space. *Peres:* Divided will be the bed of the sea and the space of the oceans, its treasures plundered, its life destroyed, and conflict and pollution rampant all over the world."

The writing is on the wall. Perhaps we still have time to heed it.

East Pacific Rise.

Heavy water plant, Glace Bay, Canada.

⧘ Chapter 1 ⧘
MARGINAL MINING

There are many ways of experiencing an ocean. We may watch it from shore, lulled by its endless rhythm, the roll and roar of the surf, "its sacred battering of fortress earth." As *Homo sapiens* returns to the sea, we experience the ocean more and more from boats and ships, each of us the center of a big blue circle that moves with us as we move.

Ever since Alexander the Great lowered himself in a glass sphere into the depths of the sea, or since the first pearl divers went about their business thousands of years ago, we have experienced the strange underwater world—intoxicated, physically and spiritually, with the impression that we are flying or dreaming.

We have seen the oceans from high-flying planes: the ships look like tiny bugs and the white crests of the waves appear frozen. We have seen them from outer space: most of the Earth appears as a single sea, the color that makes it the Blue Planet.

One of the strangest ways, however, to experience the ocean is from way down, below the seabed, from "the subsoil thereof."

We take our place on a roller-coaster-like train: the one that takes the miners to work on Wall 7 East in the Lingan Colliery, Cape Breton, Canada. We are all dressed in overalls, with big rubber boots and hard hats with headlights attached. We carry the batteries in our belts, together with a supply of oxygen, just in case. We all carry ski gloves and goggles of clear shatterproof glass. The train takes off from a little station hall. From

it we can see the sea, which appears sulky and leaden, as though it did not really approve of what we are doing. The train starts. There is no driver. A door opens in front of us and closes behind, and down we go. We travel gently at first but soon pick up speed until we reach 40 kilometers per hour, which seems rather racy. The clatter is deafening. It is dark, except for the small beams of light from some of the miners' hats. A cold wind lashes our faces. I think of ghost-train rides in Disneyland.

"Don't worry," shouts the foreman, sitting next to me, above the din. "When the train goes faster than 40 kilometers, the brakes go on automatically."

We are traveling 2.5 kilometers out from the coast under the sea, at 500 meters below sea level. The ceiling above us is about 400 meters thick. The sea above us is an excellent fishing ground. As our train races on, lobsters dance their courtship pas-de-deux above our heads.

At last we arrive. A door opens and closes behind us. In front stretches an endless gallery. It is easily passable for part of its length; other parts are cluttered with pipes, machinery, and rubble. We clamber over the hurdles, walking at a brisk pace, straddling the rail tracks. Miners with soot-blackened faces sit on rocks or rubble and silently eat their sandwiches. There are 1,100 miners. We walk for miles. Above us, the sea grass drifts quietly on its way.

Wall 7, glistening black in the glare of our headlamps, is about 200 meters wide.

The ceiling of the "room" in which the mining takes place, only a few meters high, is supported by a line of hydraulic supports made in Germany. The coal shearer also comes from Germany. It pulls itself up and down the face on a strong chain while cutting coal and loading it into the face conveyor. As the coal is cut, the conveyor and roof supports are advanced by double-acting hydraulic rams. The ceiling behind collapses, and the whole "room" is moved forward. Perhaps the school of small fish that is swimming above us senses the tremor. Perhaps they stop, startled, and reel around, their motions marvelously synchronized by the Great Choreographer. They slide away in the opposite direction.

Methane levels in the mine are continuously monitored, and warning beepers sound as soon as the level rises. The air circulation is excellent. A cool breeze meets us wherever we go. The coal face is sprayed with water while being cut, to keep the dust down. Yet our faces are black; and black, alas, are the lungs of too many of the miners down here.

Most of them are the sons of miners who were themselves the sons of miners, out there on that beautiful Cape Breton island. They could have been lobster fishermen. They could have cultivated oysters. But they come from generations of miners, passing from father to son the hard life of digging coal, until quite recently with pickaxes and shovels, 200 fathoms below the sea. A hundred years ago, subsea mining was more hazardous than seafaring, which was hazardous enough. And, as among the sailors, lore and legend luxuriated among the miners, the dead beckoning to those who were to die. Preceding a disaster, so legend tells us, cries for help and sounds of falling rock might be heard in the mines. The ghosts of dead miners and coal trains drawn by phantom white horses might be seen; the rats would leave the mine as they would a sinking ship; and the colliery might be filled with a sweet perfume emanating from "death flowers" visible only to those who were to die.

Disasters today are few and far between, and the machines do marvels. The sanitary conditions are much improved. Too many miners, however, still suffer from black lung. If they wore masks, the foreman observes, they would avoid this crippling illness. But the miners choose not to wear masks because to do so would interfere with their chewing of tobacco, one of the few pleasures they have down here, 200 fathoms below the sea.

They bring up 1,100 to 1,400 tons of coal per hour, 24 hours a day. The coal is 300 million years old, and at Cape Breton, there are some 60 to 80 million tons of it.

Worldwide, the production of coal from the subsoil of the ocean floor has been estimated at about 34 million tons annually. The main producers are Australia, Chile, Turkey, Japan, Great Britain, and Canada. Japan, which has over 8,000 undersea coal miners and produces almost 10 million tons of coal from the oceans annually, has found an interesting solution to the problem of mining well away from the shore. The Japanese build artificial islands from which they drive their shafts into the seabed. At Ariake Bay in western Kyushu, the mine shaft, about 6.5 kilometers from shore, penetrates some 700 meters below sea level.

Cities, with their industries, airports, railways, and highways, have grown most rapidly when situated near the coast, where they can take advantage of coastal plains, river mouths, and estuaries. There is an abundance of cooling water for industry and an increase in the options for waste disposal. There are the economies of marine transportation. The oceans, it seems, are able to nurture terrestrial life as well as marine life, both concentrated in the narrow band where near-shore waters meet land. New cities, and the infrastructure required to support them, are today quite literally rising from the sea. They are the product of man's determination—a determination exercised with ever greater ingenuity—to capture and use the resources of the sea. The cities both live off and are made of these resources.

Besides the coal, there is offshore oil and gas to satisfy the city's energy needs. (These are discussed in Chapter 2.) We know that drinking water will come increasingly from the sea (as indicated in Chapter 5). But the city itself, materially, is more and more a product of the sea. The sand and gravel and cement for building houses and roads may come from the sea; the glass for windows and a variety of industrial and domestic uses may come from the quartz sands on the beaches; and salt, soda, magnesia, bromine, chlorine, ammonia, or heavy water may be the basis of its chemical industries (Figure 4). These minerals are fairly universal in the sea, and the absence of transportation costs, because of immediate local use, makes their extraction economical.

In fact, the extraction of sand and gravel has increased spectacularly over the past half-century. In Great Britain, for instance, the annual demand for these materials increased from 15 million tons in 1915 to over 200 million tons in 1980. Offshore production more than trebled during the 1960s alone. The 16 million tons of sand and gravel taken every year from the sea, at a value of some £30 million, now accounts for about 15 percent of total UK production. Other industrial countries are not lagging behind. By far the largest producer and consumer of offshore sand and gravel today is Japan, at 41 million tons annually. Denmark, Holland, and the United States follow. Total world production is on the order of 86 million tons, with an aggregate value of about $200 million.

The technology poses no problems. The material is generally lifted by suction dredgers (like vacuum cleaners) from a depth of no more than 30 meters. But the displacement of 86 million tons of matter from sea to land, year after year, may certainly cause some long-term changes and disturbances in world ecology. There could be changes in shorelines, river mouths, currents, temperatures, climates, upwellings, and in the distribution of living resources—changes about which we still know so little and probably will never know enough. Such changes may defeat the very purpose we pursued while generating them.

This applies not only to the dredging of sand and gravel; it also applies, to a large extent, to the extraction of other minerals and metals and to marginal mining in general. The physical impact of dredging may be compounded by chemical impacts resulting from the various metallurgical processes that may be involved. The physical consequences of substantial dredging may also interfere with other uses of the coastal area. Shipping lanes may be affected; cables and pipelines may be disturbed.

Large-scale dredging operations may interfere with marine life in a variety of ways. Bottom dwellers in the dredging area will be physically destroyed, crushed, or sucked up. Toxic gases and metals released from the subsurface of the seafloor may kill, sicken, or genetically affect other animals and plants. Eutrophic effects may result from the release of nutrients—such as phosphorus or nitrogen—from sediments, causing algae "blooms" which kill other forms of life in the area. Water turbidity, an inevitable consequence of dredging, has manifold ecological consequences. It interferes with the feeding of filter feeders, such as mussels and oysters. It reduces light penetrability and planktonic productivity. This in turn may affect the whole food chain. At the same time, it reduces oxygen production and in the long run causes deoxidation of sea water. Finally, when the dust settles, it may choke hatching fish eggs and bury spat and larvae. Offshore ecosystems are very complex and in many cases we may simple not know what we are doing.

Cement for roads and houses contains calcareous shells, which have a number of industrial uses. They can be used in the manufacture of paper, soda ash, agricultural lime, poultry feed, and other products. Along the coast of Texas and Louisiana, roads, driveways, and parking lots are largely paved with material made of calcareous shells. There are dead shell reefs and living reefs on the continental shelf which are "mined" for this purpose. The United States had a shell production in 1977 of 12.3 million tons at a value of $33.5 million. Iceland, France, and Fiji rank next as important producers.

Corals are also mined widely—from southern Europe (France, Italy) to North Africa, from Hawaii to Sri Lanka. Coral is used for the manufacture of ornamental objects and jewelry. It is also used for industrial purposes, especially for the production of agricultural lime. In some parts of the world, coral mining has a long history and continues to make use of traditional primitive technologies. In Sri Lanka, for instance, coral miners wearing quaint-looking face masks with openings only for eyes and mouth, armed with knives, staves, or crowbars, dive down to the coral reef during low tide. Frequently they carry heavy stones to enable them to sink faster. Once on the reef, they pry the coral loose with their primitive tools and throw it into a small basket. Then they rise to their raft, where they exchange their load for another heavy stone to drag them down again. This they continue to do until the raft is so heavily laden that it begins to sink. They then tow it to the shore, where the coral is baked in an ancient kiln. Two days of baking are required to transform the coral into lime.

In contrast, the newly industrialized Taiwanese use a two-man submersible to comfortably and efficiently harvest their precious pink coral.

Aragonite is another dredged mineral that goes into the making of cement, lime, steel, glass, pulp, and paper as well as other industrial products. It deserves special mention because of the peculiar circumstances of its extraction. The world's largest offshore aragonite mine is Ocean Cay, southeast of the Bimini Islands in the Bahamas. Ocean Cay is a 198-acre artificial island, formed entirely by sand dredged from the seafloor. The aragonite is suction-dredged, dehydrated, and stockpiled on the island, at a rate of about 1,500 metric tons per hour. The reserve has been estimated at 70 to 90 billion tons!

Ocean Cay emerged from shallow seas, no more than 2 to 3 meters deep. Where dredging has taken place over the past ten years, the water depth has doubled to 5 to 6 meters. Operations are continuously monitored, and buffer zones may have to be established where dredging will be prohibited so as to protect fishing grounds.

Other materials for the building of the city may be available from the sea. Metals and minerals may be diffused in the sands of beaches, and in the beaches submerged when the last ice age ended, the glaciers melted, and the level of the oceans rose. These metals and minerals were carried by rivers from eroding mountains, through the plains, to the sea. Waves working over the sands often separate the metals and minerals from the sand and gravel, thus generating concentrated placer deposits of tin, gold, platinum, or diamonds and a number of other minerals. These can be recovered by dredging with line buckets, scrapers, grabbers, and most frequently, suction dredgers.

"Conventional" dredges can work to a depth of about 15 meters. For greater depths, a curious kind of dredge has been invented, the so-called walking dredge. This consists of a platform and suction dredge. While at work, the platform stands on three legs on the ocean floor. When work on a particular site has been completed, the platform "walks" to the next site, by lifting one leg at a time and rotating on the other two. It walks at a speed of 8 meters per hour. Such walking dredges have worked successfully at a depth of 23 meters. The expectation is that they can go much deeper.

About 6 percent of the world's tin production is dredged offshore in the form of cassiterite sands. The largest mines are in Southeast Asia, where offshore tin production is a big and expanding industry. In 1971 four dredgers, with a capacity of 260,000 cubic meters per month, were operating off the coast of Thailand. There were ten dredges with an even larger capacity operating in the Indonesian offshore. The value of tin pro-

5. Hard minerals of the offshore

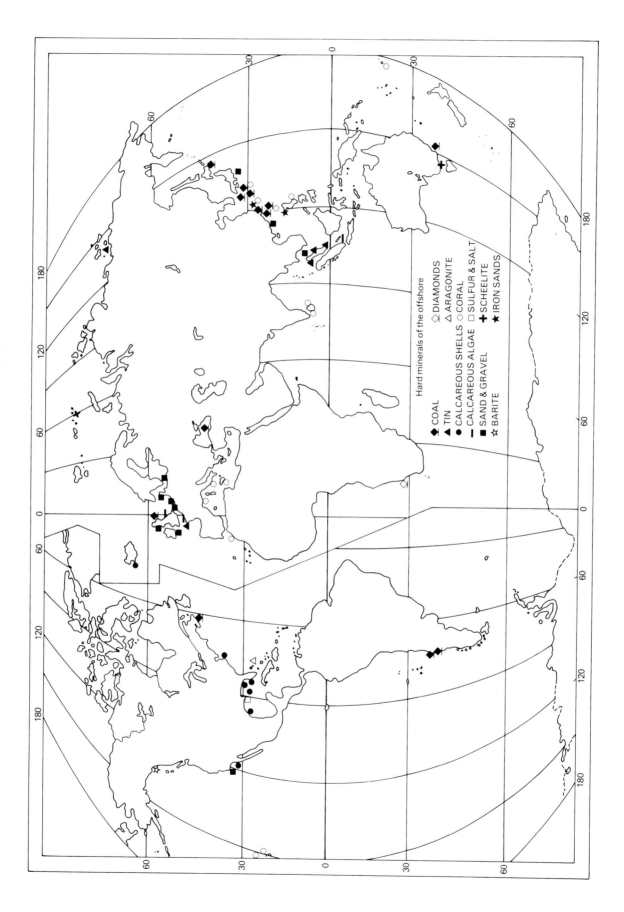

Hard minerals of the offshore

♦ COAL	◇ DIAMONDS
▲ TIN	△ ARAGONITE
● CALCAREOUS SHELLS	○ CORAL
― CALCAREOUS ALGAE	□ SULFUR & SALT
■ SAND & GRAVEL	✚ SCHEELITE
☆ BARITE	★ IRON SANDS

duced in this way in Southeast Asia has been estimated at about $30 million annually.

The Soviet Union is mining cassiterite tin ore in the Vankina Guba, a small bay in the Laptev Sea. Soviet scientists have developed a remarkable arsenal of sea-mining tools. They include splendid specially constructed prospecting ships, a robot with a deep-sea television camera, a manipulator, a remote-control system for gathering samples from the deep ocean floor, and a self-propelled bottom crawler with octopus-like tentacles capable of raking in sand from the ocean floor and sucking it up. As Ruth Linebaugh, an expert on ocean mining in the Soviet Union, describes it, "The metal-bearing sand is then drawn through a hose for primary processing, and the useless sand is returned to fill in a previously worked area. By this means, since no chemicals are used in primary processing, mining operations can conceivably be carried out without disturbing the ocean ecology."

The Soviet Union is also using nuclear-powered dredges for its cassiterite tin mining operations. With these dredges, mining can be carried out all the year round, even in Arctic conditions. Extensive dredging operations have been carried out by Soviet scientific and industrial enterprises in the Baltic Sea, the Black Sea, the Sea of Okhot, the Arctic, and the Sea of Japan. The largest tin ore dredge, however, was built by the Japanese. It is a continuous-belt dredge (line buckets) capable of working at a depth of 4,000 meters.

Cassiterite tin ore mining is thus practiced worldwide. Where weather conditions are favorable and seas are calm, offshore mining has considerable advantages over land-based operations. In Southeast Asia, production costs per ton have been estimated to be about 30 percent cheaper than on land. According to still more optimistic Soviet calculations, offshore mining costs are only one-half to one-fifth those of mining on land.

Other minerals recovered by dredging from heavy sands and placers, with their quantities and values, are listed in Table 5. Important locations of offshore mineral resources are given in Table 6 and Figure 5.

Ilmenite, rutile, and zircon have been extracted on a large scale from heavy sands by Australia during the past ten years. Ilmenite and rutile are lustrous black minerals containing iron and titanium, and titanium is a strategic mineral important in the manufacture of aircraft, satellites, and chemical equipment. Zircon is a silicate of zirconium, a golden brown or reddish transparent mineral used as a gem. It is also of strategic importance since the zirconium it contains is used in alloys, ceramics, and cladding for nuclear fuel in reactors. Of the 1971 world production, Australia produced 95 percent of the rutile, 25 percent of the ilmenite, and 87 percent of the zircon.

Other sites of heavy-mineral sands have been discovered off the coasts of Java and Bali in Indonesia, the coasts of Luzon in the Philippines and of Japan, and on the beaches of northern Taiwan. Impressive quantities were found in the 1970s off the coast of Mozambique by the German research ship *Valdivia*. At a water depth of between 20 and 500 meters, the heavy sands were found to contain about 50 million tons of recoverable ilmenite, 1.5 million tons of rutile, and 4 million tons of zircon. These reserves add up to ten times the present annual production of the industrialized world! Again, more research and development is needed. As Erich Blissenbach, a senior scientist at Preussag AG, points out, the Mozambique coast is exposed to tropical storms, and at present no technology is available to mine these minerals from a depth beyond 15 meters. Blissenbach places his hopes in the "walking dredge."

Some metals and minerals on the continental shelves and margins are of biological origin. That is, these minerals are concentrated in the shells of tiny animals (diatoms), which die and sink to the bottom where they form a dark-colored organic ooze. The ooze fossilizes through the ages. Metalliferous oozes occur mostly on shallow shelves where

Table 5: Production Value of Offshore Minerals

	Production Value (1972)	% Value from Ocean	Projected Production Value (1980)
SUBSURFACE SOLUBLE MINERALS AND FLUIDS:			
Petroleum (oil and gas)	10,300	18	90,000*
Frasch sulphur	25	33	
Salt	.1		
Potash (production expected in 1980s)	None	...	
Geothermal energy	None	...	
Freshwater springs	35†	...	
SURFICIAL DEPOSITS:			
Sand and gravel	100	< 1	
Lime shells	35	80	
Gold	None	...	2,000‡
Platinum	None	...	
Tin	53	7	
Titanium sands, zircon, and monazite	76	20	
Iron sands	10	< 1	
Diamonds (closed down in 1972)	None	...	
Precious coral	7	100	
Barite	1	3	
Manganese nodules (production expected by early 1980s)	...	...	
Phosphorite	None	...	
SUBSURFACE BEDROCK DEPOSITS:			
Coal	335	2	
Iron ore	17	< 1	
EXTRACTED FROM SEA WATER:			
Salt	173	29	
Magnesium	75	61	
Magnesium compounds	41	6	
Bromine§	< 20	30	
Fresh water	51	...	2,000‡
Heavy water	27	20	
Others (potassium salts, calcium salts, and sodium sulphate)	1	...	
Uranium	None	...	
TOTAL	...	...	94,000

SOURCE: G. J. S. Govett and M. H. Govett, *World Mining Supplies.*
Note: Total production value of nonpetroleum commodities = $691 million; total from sea water = $388 million.
* Projections indicate that offshore production by 1980 will probably at least triple the 1972 output rate of 9.5 million barrels of oil and 17 billion (10^9) cu ft of gas per day and crude-oil price will probably be stabilized around $10 per barrel.
† Sea water plant at Freeport, Texas, closed down in late 1969 (U.S. Bureau of Mines, *Mineral Year Book 1971* (Washington, D.C.: U.S. Bureau of Mines, 1973), 1:233).
‡ Also assuming an average 30 percent increase of raw minerals.
§ More than 200 million gallons of fresh water are recovered per day from submarine springs in Argolis Bay, Greece, but only a small portion of the produced water is utilized.

Table 6: Location of Offshore Mineral Resources

Mineral	Geographical Location	Water Depth (Feet)
Sand and gravel	Atlantic and Pacific coasts, US	< 100
Glass and foundry sand	Atlantic and Pacific coasts, US	< 200
Magnetite	Australia; India; Japan; Pacific coast, US	100–400
Glauconite	Pacific coast, US	30–6,000
Rutile	Australia; Atlantic coast, US	< 100
Zircon	Australia	< 100
Tin	Malaysia; Indonesia; Thailand; Alaska; Great Britain	< 400
Silver	Pacific and Alaskan coasts, US	< 400
Gold	Pacific and Alaskan coasts, US	< 400
Platinum	Pacific and Alaskan coasts, US	< 400
Diamonds	Southwest Africa	< 200
Manganese	Atlantic and Pacific Oceans; Mediterranean Sea	4,000–18,000
Phosphorite	Atlantic and Pacific Oceans, US; Australia; Africa	100–4,000
Coal	Canada; Great Britain; Japan	< 400
Monazite	South India; Sri Lanka	0–200
Shell	Gulf and Pacific coasts, US; Iceland	< 100
Sulfur	Gulf coast, US	< 100

SOURCE: J. L. Goodier, "How to Mine Minerals," p. 46.

upwellings make the water biologically productive. Oozes may contain uranium, vanadium, molybdenum, nickel, and other metals which could be mined commercially, assuming that more research and development succeeds in perfecting technologies for concentrating these metals.

Uranium-rich oozes were discovered at the bottom of the Black Sea during the 1970s. These are already being mined in a joint venture between a Soviet state enterprise and the government of Turkey.

Uranium in remarkably high concentrations—a thousand to a hundred thousand times greater than that occurring in sea water or average sediments!—together with mo-lybdenum and vanadium has been discovered along the coast of southwest Africa in a number of shallow basins. Covering a total of 19,000 square kilometers, the basins have a depth of up to 15 meters.

Another mineral that has been discovered in vast quantities on the continental margin (and also in the abyssal ocean floor) is ocean phosphorite (P_2O_5). Like potassium (see Chapter 6), this is immensely important to the fertilizer industry. Occurring in such forms as phosphatic mud banks, sands, pellets, oolites, clumps, and nodules, it can be simply crushed and applied as a fertilizer. The total amount recoverable from the oceans has been estimated at 30 billion tons, which at present rates of consumption constitutes a thousand years' supply! Ocean phosphorite has been discovered off southern California, where over 29,000 acres have been leased for phosphate mining. Significant reserves have also been found off Latin America, Australia, Spain, and northwestern and southern Africa, off the coast of Guinea, and on the Agulhas Plateau.

Extensive exploration has been carried out in recent years by Preussag's *Sonne* on the Chatham Rise off the east coast of New Zealand, where very large phosphate nodule deposits have been identified at an average depth of about 400 meters. Estimates of the deposits run in excess of 100 million tons. And since New Zealand agriculture is the most phosphate-intensive in the world, the deposits can be expected to find a ready market. To replace current imports with domestic seabed production would save the country some $60 million annually.

Phosphate nodules look black and may reach a diameter of 15 centimeters. The technology for mining them is basically the same as that for the mining of manganese nodules, except that it is obviously a lot easier to mine at a depth of 500 meters than at a depth of 5,000! (See Chapter 3.)

Marginal mining, as we have seen, comprises:

• Minerals deep below the ocean floor which can be extracted by tunneling from shore or from artificial islands. While in the past tin and copper have been extracted from offshore mines, today it is almost exclusively coal that is mined by this method.
• Surficial minerals and metals, that is, resources on the surface of the seafloor, even though they may be buried under more recent sediments. These minerals may be in the form of incrustations, or they may be loosely diffused in sands, placers, or oozes. They may be of inorganic origin, like the sands of placers, carried by rivers from eroding mountainsides; or they may be of organic origin, like the calcareous shells and metalliferous oozes, formed by detrital diatoms. These metals and minerals can be recovered

by various forms of dredging in deeper and deeper waters.

Tunneling and dredging are not the only ways of extracting marginal minerals. Pumping is a well-tried method, but its role today is a minor one. It has been used mainly for extracting sulphur from beneath the seabed, especially on the Louisiana shore in the Gulf of Mexico. Increasingly strict environmental legislation, which has regulated sulphur emissions from smelting operations, has brought sulphur mining largely to an end. This situation is a beautiful example of the fact that pollution is basically *waste*. It serves also to show that, as the Chinese put it, the "three evils of pollution"—waste solids, waste fluids, and waste gases—can be converted into "three advantages," that is, into resources for new production. But if this desirable state is to be achieved, an industry can no longer be considered as a separate entity, producing a single commodity at the greatest possible financial profit. Rather, it must be seen as part of a more comprehensive production system designed to benefit the community as a whole. That change along these lines is possible is shown in the smelting industry. Smelting operations, aimed at maximizing profits from metallurgical processing, used to pollute the atmosphere with their sulphuric emissions. Under the new legislation introduced in many industrialized countries, these emissions are now captured. In 1977 they accounted for a sulphur production of 5,589,000 tons in the United States alone, at a value of roughly $140 million. It is obvious that this "advantage" of production is greater than the cost of curbing the "evil" of pollution, even though it is not the smelting industry that directly nets the profit. This technology has created a glut on the sulphur market, and offshore sulphur pumping has declined as a result. However, one mine is still in operation: Grand Isle mine, owned by the Freeport Sulphur Company, off the coast of Louisiana. The mine consists of a number of platforms connected by bridges, in a water depth of about 15 meters. Production in the 1970s averaged

1.3 million tons annually, at a value of approximately $36 million.

Another way of extracting marginal minerals—although it is not yet practiced—is by nuclear explosion. This might be applied to ore deposits that formed millions of years ago as metalliferous muds near the central rift of a growing ocean and then moved outward as the seafloor kept spreading. Over the millions of years these deposits may have been covered by hundreds of meters of shelf sediments and, under this pressure, turned into hard rock. As Erich Blissenbach points out, "A mining technique is not yet available. However, depending on the size and grade of such metallic ore, it could be envisaged to apply nuclear devices for a fragmentation of the solid rock and then use solution mining. It is necessary that the ore deposits are no less than 400 meters below the seabed to assure containment of the nuclear explosion products. . . . The process is claimed to have even environmental advantages because there is no disposal of tailings nor smelting of concentrates and a minimum disturbance of the seabed. The solution would be entirely recycled and there should be no seepage loss."

In 1981 discoveries were made by the U.S. National Atmospheric and Oceanic Administration (NOAA) which may revolutionize ocean mining and, at least temporarily, detract attention from the nodules of the deep ocean floor.

A group of scientists led by NOAA's Senior Scientist, Russian-born Alex Malahoff, descended in the famous submersible *Alvin* to produce a detailed geological map of the Galapagos ridge extending for several hundred kilometers from the Galapagos islands. Two active rift valleys were discovered, separated by a huge rocky mountain 7 kilometers long, 100 meters high, and 600 meters wide. This rock, in turn, is bounded north and south by "normal faults," that is, breaks caused by a shifting of the earth's crust. These are the sites of recent hydrothermal activity, with volcanic chimneys, or

"smokers," around which rare forms of life have been found.

Four sites of massive polymetallic sulfide ore deposits were mapped. The largest one, on the southern end of the mountain, forms a metalliferous ridge 35 meters high, 150 meters wide, and 1 kilometer long. It contains several million tons of polymetallic sulfides (iron, copper, silver, cadmium, vanadium, molybdenum, manganese, lead, cobalt, and zinc). The water depth is 2,600 meters, about half as deep as the manganese nodule deposits. The metal content appears

DRILLING/MAINTENANCE VESSEL

FLOWLINES / T F L
CONTROL LINES

SATELLITE WELL
CHRISTMAS TREE

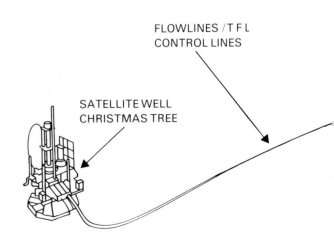

6. The underwater manifold center production system

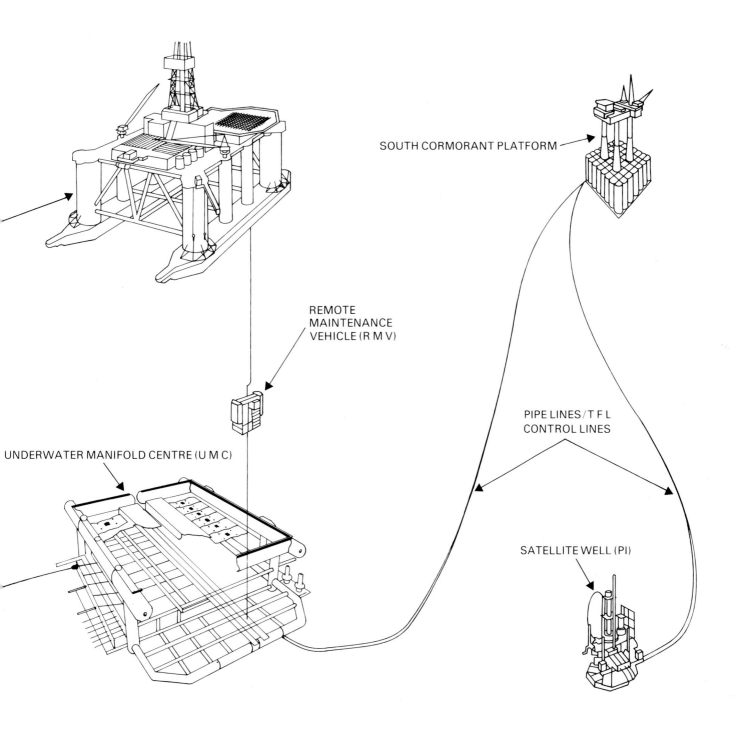

SOUTH CORMORANT PLATFORM

REMOTE
MAINTENANCE
VEHICLE (R M V)

UNDERWATER MANIFOLD CENTRE (U M C)

PIPE LINES / T F L
CONTROL LINES

SATELLITE WELL (PI)

to be very much higher than that of the nodules—60 percent rather than 2 to 3 percent. Although caution is called for, since exploration has only just begun and sampling is wholly inadequate, the projected costs of mining and processing appear comparatively low.

Similar discoveries have been made off the coasts of Oregon and Washington in the U.S. and off British Columbia in Canada. Malahoff himself described his discovery as "a dramatic turning point" in the history of mining.

It took a thousand years to map the world the way we know it: the contours of continents, the course of rivers, the height of mountain peaks; boundaries, populations, urban concentrations; resources, communications, industries. As generations of geographers and cartographers added pages to terrestrial atlases, they left the oceans blank or marked them with a symbolic sea monster, designations which indicated not only that the oceans were unexplored, but also that man was ignorant about and even in awe of the sea.

The seas were painted blue, a blue that stood for depth and silence. Despite the rich human experience with the oceans accumulated over the past millennia, it was only during the twentieth century that mapmakers began to dilute and differentiate their ocean blue. Mountain ranges and valleys, shelves, plateaus, currents, and upwellings have broken the seascape monotony. Seaweed varieties and concentrations and the densities of fish populations, marine mammals and various waterfowl; shipping routes and shallows, ports and harbors, roadsteads, rigs; and sunken cities and the sites of naval battles have gradually appeared on the map. The mineral resources, on shelves and ridges and on the abyssal plain, are being recorded as they are being discovered. But only now.

The mapping of minerals begins with a general geological survey, based, in most cases nowadays, on satellite and air photographs which clearly delineate coastlines,

mangrove swamps, and reefs. Next comes the charting of sea bottom morphology by echo-sounding from ships. This provides a set of geographic maps showing surface morphology. After this, a set of geologic surface maps is made. These are based on collections and analyses of surface samples or rocks and sediments dredged from the seafloor. The mapping of offshore placers is greatly facilitated by knowledge of terrestrial geology and the mineral composition of hinterland mountains, and the study of their erosion and transportation and the reconstruction of sea levels during earlier geological periods.

When surface geology has been determined, subsoil structures can be assayed by geophysical methods. These methods include seismic air guns, gravimetry (the measurement of the weight and density of samples and the determination of the earth's gravitational pull at different places), and magnetometry (the determination of the earth's magnetic field during various geological periods). Geochemical analyses of soil and water samples also contribute to this phase of mapping.

Improved and more detailed knowledge of the history of ocean basins, of rifting, and of continental drift will facilitate the search for minerals. The experience of marine scientists suggests that it may be wasteful to search for one mineral at a time. Seafloor charting, sediment mapping, soil investigations, seismic surveys, may lead to hydrocarbon development, but they benefit other marine exploration and research as well. As Erich Blissenbach explains, "In certain cases of marine reconnaissance work, the search for oil and gas can be combined with that for hard minerals."

Ocean mapping has lagged behind terrestrial mapping by several hundred years. By the year 2000, perhaps, the ocean atlas will be as rich and complex as today's terrestrial atlas, mirroring man's multifarious activities in the seas, his knowledge, cultivation and utilization of all their resources, his return to the sea where all life began.

Opposite above:
The *Statfjord A* platform in the North Sea.

48

Opposite below:
The *Statfjord A* platform in the North Sea.

The *Statfjord B* platform.

Top:
Launching a free-fall grab in manganese
nodule exploration.

Above:
Detail of the flotation plant installed on
SEDCO 445. Air is injected into the seawater-
sediment mixture to form a foam containing
base metal–bearing sulfides at the surface.

Opposite:
Heavy box grab corer.

Box corer with heat flow measuring unit.

The SEDCO 445.

Overleaf:
Oil drilling platforms in an unfamiliar setting.
Science fiction has already become scientific
fact in the exploitation of the oceans' hydrocarbon resources.

⦚ Chapter 2 ⦚
DEEPSEA SAGA

The title of this chapter does not augur more mythology. *Deepsea Saga* is the name, not of a legend, but of an oil exploration platform in the Statfjord field, 160 kilometers from Bergen in the Norwegian offshore. We shall pay it a visit.

Our journey starts at Bergen's Flesland airport. The helicopter that is to take us to the platform rises like an elevator, then veers northwest over fjords and coves, rocky islets and woods, and small white houses, out over the blue open sea.

It is 7:30 in the morning. The helicopter is taking a new shift of about twenty crew members back to the platform.

The helicopter is quite comfortable and steady in spite of high North Sea winds. We all wear "survival suits"—heavily quilted waterproof orange overalls, and life jackets over them, with whistles and lights. In case of emergency, we could survive for five hours in the autumnal cold of the North Sea. That, we are assured by the foreman, is long enough to be picked up in this intensively surveilled and navigated area.

The flight takes one hour. On arrival we descend, again elevator-like, straight onto *Deepsea Saga*'s octagonal heliport. The surface is covered with wide-mesh netting to prevent slipping. A few men stand by, ready to instantly cover the heliport with chemical foam in the event of fire.

Resting on eight sturdy pillars on its two submersed pontoons, *Deepsea Saga* is like an enormous ship with three decks and a tower. The comfortable cabins housing the crew of

about seventy men are on the middle deck. Here also are most of the offices, the monitoring, control, and computer rooms, and a lounge with excellent Scandinavian furniture, well-filled magazine racks, and a television set. The mess room is also here, where four abundant meals are served daily from a rather spectacular kitchen that works around the clock. Catering for offshore rigs has become big business. Eating provides the main entertainment for oil workers isolated in this stark and dangerous environment for two weeks at a time, working around the clock in long and hard twelve-hour shifts. "That's where the quality of catering comes in," an advertisement of Norske Chalk Catering announces. "Pleasant breaks for good meals are essential in more than one way. . . . They are the grease that prevents the machinery from squeaking."

The men drift in in ones and twos. Although they are cleaned up and dressed in civilian clothes, their faces betray their fatigue. There is not much conversation, nor any other manifestation of joy, as they tuck into the enticing *smorgasbord*.

Next to the mess room is the movie theater, where films are shown three times a day. "Sex and violence," one of the men said, rather contemptuously, though while I was there the films that were showing did not bear out his judgment.

Food and films exhaust the list of entertainments. There is no Ping-Pong, no exercise bicycle or other sports facility, even though much of the work on the rig is somewhat sedentary, involving monitoring and charting.

A hundred meters or so away is a small ship. It is always there: our standby in the event that anything goes wrong on the rig. The ship is heaving and rocking in the waves. Our platform, anchored with eight heavy chains (each weighing about 15 tons) to the ocean floor some 200 meters below, is steady. Sometimes, however, in heavy storms, the chains break. Then the thrusters are activated to keep the platform steady.

The thrusters are powered by eight diesel engines located on the lower level of the platform. With 10,000 horsepower each, there is enough power for self-propulsion, and *Deepsea Saga* can travel—slowly—alone. Generally, however, she is towed over longer distances.

In the machine room the noise is deafening. We wear earplugs under our hard hats, which must be worn everywhere on board. We escape to the huge desalination plant, a couple of doors away, which produces fresh water for this floating community. Close by is the "mud room," where mud is processed with various chemicals stored in rack after rack of sacks. It is used in drilling to control pressure and to clean the well.

We walk across the lowest deck and enter the shed of *Subsea Dolphin,* a relative newcomer to the platform. *Subsea Dolphin* is a handsome little submarine, just big enough to hold one man lying on his stomach. He has a wide glass window in front of him and a control console which he uses to manipulate the battery-powered ship and the artificial arms in front of the window. With it, he is able to perform simple repair work on the rig.

Until quite recently divers were sent down with only scuba gear to carry out repairs by hand. Many of them died: more, it seems, than the industry cares to admit. Lured by the promise of high financial rewards and perhaps by the challenge of defying the elements, many went down only to perish. Though there are still problems with

the *Dolphin,* it has made underwater repair work considerably safer.

We walk across the lower deck, around the "moon well," the opening through which the drilling pipe reaches from the tower into the depths of the ocean floor. The drill works day and night. When the going is good, it can drill as much as 30 meters in an hour; when it's hard, maybe 1 meter or 2, or none. Every 13 meters, the process is interrupted. The pipe string is unscrewed and a new segment of pipe is inserted by three workers with the help of powerful winches.

The winches make strange noises, like the song of the whale alternating with the wailing of babies. Another piece of electronic gear, which records water depth and time, emits sequences of high-pitched electronic flutelike sounds—a little motif of triads which it repeats furiously, time and again, contrapuntally to the sounds of the winch. And below it all is the rhythmic stomping of a pump. No contemporary electronic composer could comment better on the mood on the rig.

The drill bit is now 1,690 meters below the ocean floor. The pressure is rising, but blowouts are few and far between. Statistics reportedly show that the frequency of production blowouts in the Gulf of Mexico is 1 for every 2,500 well-years of production! In the North Sea, where production is more intense, statistics are as yet inconclusive. What they appear to indicate is 1 blowout every 770 well-years—still a rather soothing thought as we listen to that infernal symphony and watch the rising pressure. Adding segment after segment of pipe string, *Deepsea Saga* should reach a sub–ocean floor depth of 3,700 meters within eighty days.

The floor of the lowest deck, around the moon well, is an iron grate. Walking on it, one sees, hears, and feels an irate sea, churning, foaming, writhing against this yoke. *Deepsea Saga* would have been a myth only twenty years ago. Today it is a piece of routine technology.

While *Deepsea Saga* is exploring, a huge fixed platform, *Statfjord A,* is already intensively exploiting Norway's northernmost giant oil field. Two additional platforms, *Statfjord B* and *C,* are expected to start production in the mid-1980s.

Platform A has been described by Stat-Oil as an eighty-three-storey concrete and steel skyscraper, standing as a man-made island in the middle of the turbulent North Sea in waters 138 meters deep. "It is literally a crude oil producing and processing plant, along with a self-contained community," a community that lives on the main platform and on two satellite floating platforms 180 kilometers off the west coast of Norway.

Statfjord A started producing in the fall of 1980. Peak production should be reached sometime in 1984, only ten years after the giant Statfjord field was first discovered by Mobil Oil in 1974. On this one platform alone, peak production is expected to reach 300,000 barrels of crude a day, equivalent to an annual production of more than 15 million tons!

Statfjord A's electrical power plant generates 65 megawatts, enough to power a city of 33,000 people. With a total area of over 6 acres on its three levels, it has sufficient space to drill up to twenty wells. Sixteen have been drilled so far, the deepest reaching a depth of 3,100 meters.

About 2 kilometers from the platform is another moored structure. Called the Articulated Loading Platform, or ALP, it is connected to the platform by a pipeline. This is where the tankers are loaded with Platform A's production to carry it to the Norwegian mainland or to other parts of the world. The *Statfjord A*'s ALP is the largest in the world: 182 meters high, with a loading capacity of 60,000 barrels per hour. Adapted particularly to the harsh weather conditions of the North Sea, it allows tankers to continue loading even when the sea is high. The top part of the loading system can tilt and rotate like a weathervane so that the tanker has freedom to move with prevailing winds and currents.

Oil is formed when plant and animal debris falls to the ocean floor and decays. This debris may be of marine origin, or it may be of terrestrial origin, claimed by the ocean when its level rises at the end of a glacial period and forests and the life therein are drowned.

Organic debris is deposited as mud on the ocean floor. These organic muds are subsequently covered by thousands of meters of clays and sand. The deeper the mud is buried, the greater the pressure and the higher the temperature. Over millions of years, high temperatures transform the organic mud into oil, which begins to seep upward. When it finds suitable folds or other kinds of traps, such as layers of hard clay or rock or salt domes, an oil field is born.

Although pressure-generated high temperatures may be a sufficient explanation for the origin of an oil field, it has been shown that many oil fields actually originated in the warmer climates of the tropics and then wandered toward the poles, as the ocean floor spread and continents drifted. Indeed, much North Sea rock wandered to its present position from the equator, between 400 and 200 million years ago. The route can be reconstructed by measuring the old magnetic field direction of rocks of different ages. Geophysics and an understanding of continental drift may thus be of fundamental importance for oil exploration. Until the discovery of the Statfjord field, some experts argued that it would be useless to look for oil in the North Sea in rock formations younger than 200 million years. This was based on the assumption that oil necessarily had to have its origin in warmer climates—and the youngest formations of tropical origin in the North Sea are 200 million years old.

Oil and gas in the Statfjord field, however, is of Jurassic age and was formed approximately 150 million years ago. Hence it must have originated considerably farther north. Recoverable reserves are estimated at 470 million metric tons of oil and about 70 billion cubic meters of gas, which makes Statfjord the biggest offshore oil field in the world. If all its production were to be consumed in Norway at present and projected rates of consumption, the oil would meet the country's needs for more than fifty years.

But that, of course, is not all—far from it. Norway is exploring and exploiting other fields. In addition to Ekofish, there are Odin and Frigg, Tor, Edda and Valhall. Norway, it seems, has invoked the entire Nordic pantheon to christen its fields, perhaps in recognition of the superhuman efforts required before the fields yield their rewards. And the rewards are tremendous. The total oil and gas reserves on the Norwegian continental shelf are between 29.2 and 36.5 billion barrels of oil equivalent (approximately 3 billion tons), and estimates of proven reserves are rapidly rising.

Yet Norway, deliberate, slow, and prudent in its oil development policy, is only the second largest producer in the North Sea. The lion's share is taken by Britain. The area of Britain's offshore fields, with names like Toni and Thelma, Thistle and Heather, and the famed Forties—less awesome than their Norwegian counterparts—is twice as large as Norway's. Britain has pursued an aggressive development policy. Only ten years after the first discoveries in 1969, and barely four years after the first oil came on stream in 1974, Britain had achieved self-sufficiency in both oil and natural gas. In 1979 the UK's 181 active wells produced 1,527,520 barrels of oil a day, or almost 46 million metric tons per year. And 195 new wells were drilled in 1980.

The drilling boom has assumed unprecedented dimensions globally. "There has

British Petroleum's drilling platform *SEA Quest*, in the North Sea, 1972.

never been a period in the history of oil and gas that compares to the world wide drilling and producing boom currently underway," *World Oil* jubilated on August 15, 1980. "There's a gold rush ahead, but industry can hardly believe its eyes," Richard Shepherd commented in *Noroil* in October of the same year. As the industry penetrates farther and farther out into the oceans, including increasingly inhospitable environments, new technologies are being developed apace. The North Sea, with its storms, high waves, and rough geological substrata, is a laboratory for the development of such new technology, especially in connection with deep-water finds—too deep for conventional platforms—and with shallow-water reservoirs too limited in size to be exploited with traditional technology.

A variety of futuristic-looking gravity platforms, with tripod substructures, articulated columns oscillating around a static equilibrium position, or floating production systems, have been designed and tested. The new fixed platforms can operate in a water depth of up to 400 meters and can withstand any storm that may have piled the North Sea billows into mountains during the last one hundred years. Drilling from floating rigs in water 3,000 meters deep is already within the realm of the possible.

The latest in the way of advanced technology is the so-called Underwater Manifold Center Production System recently developed by Shell and Esso for the Cormorant Field in the UK sector of the North Sea. The Underwater Manifold Center (UMC) is installed on the ocean floor—theoretically at any depth. Covering an area about half the size of a football field, it is as tall as a four-storey building and weighs about 2,200 tons.

The UMC is capable of handling up to nine wells, which can be either drilled directly or linked to it by pipeline. It collects fluids from the production wells and conducts them through pipelines to the main platform; using tools pumped through pipelines from the platform, it distributes treated sea water from the platform into the water

injection wells to maintain reservoir pressure and thus increase production rates. Most of the components of the control systems can be replaced by remote-controlled manipulators (robots), which greatly reduces the need for divers.

This new, highly complex, and quite costly—about $1 billion—structure has been described by the Technical Director of Shell U.K. Exploration and Production as signifying "a revolution in underwater techniques and an extremely important landmark not only in North Sea history but in world oil production." Since the UMC can be operated at any depth, it makes it possible to drill in deeper and deeper waters. It also makes it possible to recover more from a well. Rather than just "creaming" the oil and moving on to the next well, the UMC is designed to extract all, or very nearly all, there is from a single well.

The industry has come a long way in a very short time. Offshore oil was first produced in 1894 in California from wells drilled from wooden wharves. Not much progress was made during the next forty years, the period that saw the rise of the great land-oil empires. In 1936 operations began in the Gulf of Mexico, culminating in the discovery of the Creole field. In 1948 the first offshore platform beyond the sight of land was completed off the coast of Louisiana in a water depth of about 16 meters.

It took the oil engineering industry nearly twenty years to develop the technology required to drill in 200 meters of water. But when that point was reached, it was as if a barrier had been broken. Drilling under 400 meters of water was accomplished in 1967, and now it can be done at practically any depth.

While the first platforms were built *in situ*, later giants were built ashore, like ships, and towed to their destination. Even here, however, there have been some interesting innovations. At Brown and Roots Anahuac, in Texas, a barge-mounted drilling rig has been constructed that can actually fly. The huge barges on which the rig is mounted form a hovercraft that is able to hover more than 1 meter above the ground. It can thus transport itself over marshes and shallows to places where no rig has yet set foot.

Proposals have also been made to directly link the exploitation of oil to the production of petrochemicals. In cases where there is insufficient gas to pipe or tanker it away but too much to flare, the raw gas could be fed into a giant floating petrochemical plant which would convert it into methanol and ammonia. Such a proposal was presented by Process Energy Services, Inc., at the 1981 Offshore Technology Conference held in Houston, Texas. Using technology presently available, the plant, it was suggested, could produce about 3,000 tons of methanol per day, which could be used as motor fuel. About 1,000 tons of ammonia would be produced at the same time. This could be utilized as an agricultural fertilizer. Although designed for calmer waters than those of the North Sea, the idea illustrates a new trend of moving oil-related industries out into the ocean, a trend aimed at linking Neptune's mines with industrial parks.

North Sea reserves rival those of the Persian Gulf, and it is in the North Sea that advances have been particularly dramatic. Developments are, however, genuinely global. Exploration extends from the balmy waters of tropical offshores in Africa and South America—especially, of course, Venezuela and Mexico—to the North Atlantic (especially Canada) and the Arctic (Canadian and Norwegian), where the battle is on against icebergs and the eternal darkness of winter and drilling is possible only from June to December.

Here, too, the Norwegians have come up with a new response: a drilling platform made of ice. The idea is not quite as new as one might think. During the Second World War there was a project to develop an unsinkable aircraft carrier, made of ice and reinforced with wood, to be kept at a temperature of −15°C by an ice machine. The model, named *Habakuk*, was calculated to withstand navigation in any climate. Ice, it

has been suggested by British scientist Nigel Calder, might become the building material for artificial ocean city islands. It is quite logical to apply this idea to oil-drilling platforms in very cold climates.

In any event, *World Oil* (April 1981) reported that an Oslo lawyer has applied for a patent to construct a platform made of ice for use in Arctic regions. The body of ice is to be wrapped in special insulating material and contained by a steel and concrete wall. The resulting platform is intended for year-round operation. During the summer months the ice will be maintained by refrigeration, which in the Arctic does not require much energy.

It is one world, and the economic incentive for the further expansion of the offshore oil industry is certainly there. Even though it is projected to grow at a much slower rate than in the past, world energy demand by the year 2000 is expected to be 65 percent higher than it is today. In spite of conservation, recession, and the substitution of other energy resources in many sectors of production and communication, oil is expected to remain the major energy source until the end of the century. Total output is estimated to increase from the 1980 level of 66 million barrels per day to about 71 million barrels per day and then to level off around the year 2000. Experts estimate recoverable conventional oil reserves to be somewhere in the area of 723 billion barrels, with 550 billion barrels available for future discoveries (*Sea Technology*, October 1983). Total reserves of conventional gas resources are estimated to be 10,500 exajoules (1 exajoule is approximately 160 million barrels of oil equivalent), of which 8,150 (that is, most of it) are said to be undiscovered (*World Oil*, August 15, 1980).

About half of this may come from the world's oceans. It has been estimated that about 50,000 square kilometers of land are likely to be oil-bearing and worthy of exploration activities. Taken together, the planet's offshore regions (shelves, margins, and rises) considered worthy of oil exploration efforts

7. Offshore exploration of nodules

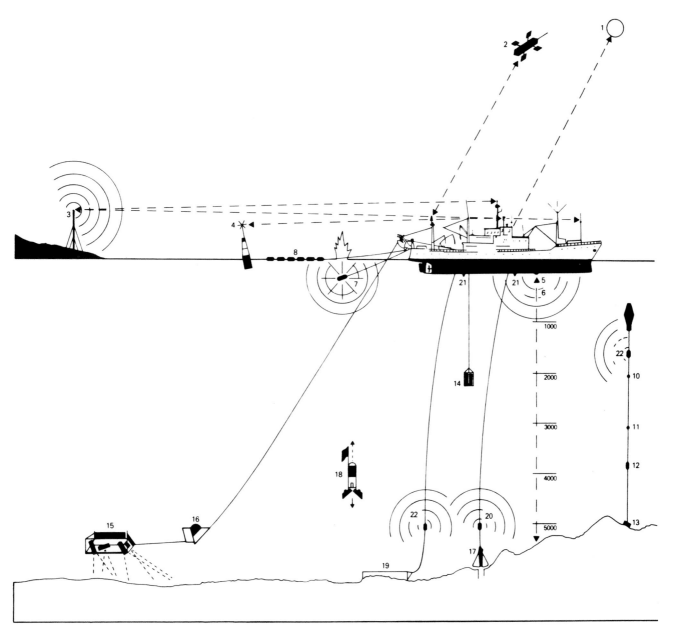

Navigation

1 Stars
2 Satellites
3 Radio navigation
4 Navigation Buoy (transponder radar)

Bathymetry

5 Narrow beam sounder (NBS)
  sediment echograph
6 Various depth recorders

Reflection Seismic

7 Airgun
8 Streamer with hydrophones
  analogue and digital registration

Oceanographic survey

9 Underwater
  measuring chain
  with localizable buoy
10 Current meter
11 Thermometer
12 Water pressure gauge
13 Cut-off anchor
14 Bathysonde (probe)
  continuous measurement of
  Temperature
  Salinity
  Sound velocity
  Pressure

Survey of Ore Deposits

15 Deep diving probe with
  TV camera still camera
  and lights
16 Stabilizing platform
17 Corer for sampling
  sediment with nodules
18 Freefall sampler
19 Bulk sampling of nodules
  for metallurgical tests

**Localization
of Launched**

20 Pinger
21 Hydrophone
22 Transponder

comprise something on the order of 80 million square kilometers.

Is this the way to go? Is this the way that we will actually go? It is a path paved with risks. "Boom," according to the dictionary, is a time of prosperity. It is also a sound, like an explosion. A deep, resonant, dark sound. A warning sound.

Oil, of course, not only comes out of the ocean. It also goes in, in quantities that may wreak havoc with life in the sea and interfere with other uses of the oceans. Although less than 10 percent of the total oil waste in the oceans comes from blowouts, this adds up to some 100,000 metric tons a year, probably more. Runoffs from rivers, industrial wastes, and automobile wastes account for half a million tons. The total amount of oil discharged into the ocean yearly between 1970 and 1980 was about 2.1 million metric tons. To this should be added an estimated 1.8 million tons of airborne hydrocarbon fallout on the sea surface. The total amount of oil and oil products contaminating the oceans has been estimated by the United Nations Environment Programme at 0.5 percent of total world production.

There has been a tendency in recent years to revise these figures downward. Economic recession, the "energy crisis," and stricter regulations on tanker traffic have kept the estimated total down to about 5 million tons annually. Long-term studies also appear inconclusive with regard to possible irreversible or even persistent consequences of oil pollution. The studies have failed to yield any concrete evidence.

It is strange, however, how statistical evidence responds to the psychological mood of the moment. In the 1970s we lived with the discovery of environmental problems. The mood of the '80s is determined by the "energy crisis." Our concern with this crisis has meant that environmental problems have been forced to take a back seat. While the fears expressed in the '70s may have been exaggerated, and the news of the imminent death of the oceans unduly pessimistic, the backlash we are currently witnessing may

prove dangerous. Five million tons of waste oil is not negligible: we would be well advised to listen to the boom in the boom!

Oil poisons marine life. Filter feeders, such as clams, oysters, scallops, and mussels, die. Edible species of fish become inedible because of the presence in oil of the chemical benzo 3-4 pyrene, which is carcinogenic.

Oil disrupts the ecosystem, not only through the destruction of juvenile forms of marine life and of the food sources of higher species, but also in subtler ways which we are just beginning to understand. Communication and orientation among marine animals often depend upon a chemical "language." Messages concerning mating, aggression, danger, and homing are coded in the chemicals they emit. This chemical language makes use, among other things, of hydrocarbons. Pollutants may interfere with the process, either by masking the natural hydrocarbons or by mimicking the natural stimuli and leading to inappropriate responses. The homing of salmon, the migration of tuna, and the schooling and mating of fish may all be disrupted. If they are, entire animal populations may be doomed to extinction.

Oil may kill through contact poisoning, through coating leading to asphyxiation, or through exposure to dissolved or colloidal toxic components at some distance in space and time from the source. The intake of small sublethal amounts of oil or oil products may reduce resistance to infections and other stress, and this may account for the death of many birds that survive immediate exposure to oil. "Rescued" birds have died after treatment, because the treatment removed, in addition to the polluting petroleum, the body oil that impregnates their feathers, thereby expelling the layer of warm air which normally maintains their body temperature in cold water. Thus, when the bird enters the water, a large amount of body heat is lost, the metabolism is slowed down, and sudden death ensues.

The breaking down of oil by bacteria in the warmer oceans consumes large quantities of oxygen. This process affects the reproduction of phytoplankton and algae. Lord Ritchie Calder describes the effect in *The Pollution of the Mediterranean:* In enclosed seas like the Mediterranean, a thin film of oil, perhaps no more than one molecule thick, could act "like a filter lens used on a camera, or in greater densities, like an opaque curtain" that can "cut off and abort the photosynthetic process and hence the release of free oxygen."

We can ignore such warnings only at great risk. We must learn to cope with them in the 1980s, the 1990s, for as long as oil remains the major energy resource. It must be dealt with at the local, the national, the regional, and the global level. And if we are to respond effectively to these new types of problems, then new forms of cooperation—among governments, international organizations, industry, and labor—will be required.

It is not only the safety of the environment that is at stake. The safety of human life is equally threatened. Some years ago, a hydrophone was improperly welded to a support strut on a leg of Norway's *Alexander Kielland* platform in the Statfjord field. A crack developed and rust began to eat its way into the support structure. One day in 1980, when the winds raced over the North Sea at 110 kilometers per hour and the waves rose a towering 6 meters, the leg collapsed and 123 men lost their lives.

Government investigations point to the need for stricter inspection of structures and equipment, more comprehensive training, including safety training, and rigorous adherence to standards. These lessons are being heeded. The Norwegian Petroleum Directorate, for instance, plans to rigidly enforce its educational standards. In the past, up to 70 percent of the drilling personnel employed on some rigs had been exempted from these standards!

Oil has become a social problem. It has created economic and political problems of unmanageable proportions.

The oil boom has had a major impact on national economies and the world economic system. While the contribution of increased oil prices to inflation has been exaggerated—other factors, like the arms race, are much more significant—the oil boom has been and remains a disruptive influence that has placed new stresses and strains on national economies. In the industrialized world the disruptions have been painful; in large parts of the nonindustrialized world they have been catastrophic. When the industry announces, "We are going to need platforms, modules, power generators, pipelines, cement, chemicals, food, ships, helicopters, support services, communication systems. Most important, we are going to need people," this may sound like good news in a time of economic depression. But it may distort the economy. Other sectors, equally vital to a nation's well-being, may be neglected, even allowed to fall into disarray.

It is in the developing countries, from the Arab world to Latin America, that oil has most strained the political and social fabric. Here, oil has been more than a disruptive influence. It has led directly to the downfall of the society that owns and controls it.

The kingdom of Portugal, the land of the great explorers and conquerors, collapsed under the weight of gold—gold that was not the fruit of indigenous labor. Gold was unsuited to the stimulation of economic growth and social development. Less fortunate neighbors, forced by adversity to mobilize their own ingenuity and labor, moved ahead, moved into the modern age, leaving behind a stagnant Portugal with an impoverished population.

In a recent study, the United Nations University draws similar conclusions with regard to the oil wealth of the Arab countries. "Power" derived from oil royalties, which are neither the product of indigenous labor nor the result of the development of local productive capacities but are rather financial assets of a "rentier" character, cannot, the study contends, be conducive to development.

The UNU study, summarized and commented on by Mohamed Sid-Ahmed in an article, "Oil on Troubled Societies," in *Develop-*

ment Forum (April 1981), draws attention to a number of apparently disparate but basically linked phenomena:

• the unprecedented influx of labor from non-oil to oil-producing Arabic countries, with the consequences attendant on the migration of labor in general;
• the breakup of family and social structures and traditions; the growth of slum and squatter settlements;
• the neglect of other sectors of the economy: countries that once exported food, like Mexico, Nigeria, and Libya, allow their agricultural sector to collapse and become dependent on imported food;
• inflation: the rich get richer and the poor get poorer, both within the oil countries and between oil and non-oil countries in the developing world;
• tensions, conflict, and violence increasingly characterize the relations between rich and poor, foreigner and native, different races and different creeds.

These are generalizations, of course, and the situation varies from country to country. Some oil-producing developing countries seem prepared to allow nature to take its course; others have recognized the dangers and are attempting to confront them. Mexico, for instance, where per capita food consumption has steadily fallen over the past decade because of poor agricultural performance, is "facing the oil-for-food specter so common among oil-developing countries," reported Alan Riding, the *New York Times* Mexico City Bureau Chief (*New York Times Magazine,* January 11, 1981). "Recognizing the absurdity of importing American food when Mexican farm laborers must go to the United States to find work, the Government has now pledged to make Mexico self-sufficient in basic grains by 1985."

In the Arab countries, the UNU study points out, the sudden exposure of the most isolated, traditional societies to alien cultural influences, sophisticated technologies, and the new spirit of consumerism has resulted

in a "culture shock," perhaps even given rise to an "identity crisis." One backlash of this identity crisis has been the dramatic resurgence of militant Islam.

None of the developing countries has yet fully come to terms with the darker sides of the oil bonanza. "Venezuela, for example, woke up in the 1970s to find it had spent fifty years of oil earnings on imported food and luxury items and had built up all too little industry," Alan Riding notes. "Saudi Arabia spent huge sums on sophisticated armaments and foreign technology but was never able to become independent of the major multinational oil companies and Western technicians. And, most worrisome, Iran tried to modernize its socio-economic structure so quickly that its rigid political system fell victim to cultural and religious rebellion."

Oil has been dubbed "black gold," and we have made reference to a "gold rush" and to the gold of the conquerors. Although we began this chapter with the promise of no further excursions into mythology, the temptation to refer, in conclusion, to one more myth is irresistible. Since the myth involves gold, and Tor and Frigg and Valhall, the nomenclature we encountered in the Norwegian oil fields, it would seem particularly appropriate. The myth is that of the Rheingold, guarded by playful maidens at the bottom of the Rhine.

The underwater scene—the fading light, the changing colors, the craggy peaks rising from the bottom—are described by Richard Wagner in *Das Rheingold* as though he had been down there in a scientific submersible; and the one eternally long halting note, from which first the Rhine motif and then all else develops, symbolizes the origin of all life from the water.

The gold is stolen from the heedless maidens by Alberich, the gnome king of the industrious Nibelungen folk. To obtain possession of the treasure, Alberich has had to forever forswear love, that is, the bright side of life. He uses the treasure to forge a ring—the Nibelungen ring. With the help of this ring he keeps his people subjected, indefatigably to slave and to mine and to forge treasures upon treasures. Finally, he wants to use the ring to subject the whole world to his dominion.

However, Alberich is tricked out of his ring by the gods in Valhall, who desperately need money; in the spirit of consumerism, they have overspent their budget by building a splendid, very costly castle, incurring a terrible balance of payments deficit in the process. Fafner, the giant, who had been contracted from abroad to construct the castle, now demands payment. Since the gods are defaulting, he resorts to terrorism and takes a hostage: Frigg's sister Freya who, to make things worse, is the divine community's gerontologist. The apples she raises keep them eternally young and vigorous. With her departure, rapid senescence is their lot. Freya's return becomes essential, and gold is needed to get her back. With cunning design, the gods in Valhall succeed in tricking Alberich out of his ring and all of his treasure. This is how Alberich parts with his wealth:

> . . . henceforth cursed be this ring.
>   Gold which gave
> me measureless might,
>   now may its magic
> deal each owner death!
>   No man shall e'er
>   own it in mirth
>   and to gladden no life
>   shall its lustre gleam.
>   May care consume
>   each sev'ral possessor
>   and envy gnaw him
>   who owns it not!
>   All shall lust
>   after its delights,
>   but none shall employ them
>   to profit him.
> To its master giving no gain,
> aye the murd'rer's brand it shall bring.
>   To death he is fated,
> its fear on his fancy shall feed;
>   though long he live

> shall he languish each day,
>   the treasure's lord
>   and the treasure's slave
>   *   *   *
> So the Nibelung blesses his ring!

Who the Alberich was who put his curse on the black gold that the ocean made and that now slumbers under its waves we do not know. Let us hope that we learn to cope with it more successfully than did the gods, who after the vicissitudes of a couple of generations, twilighted under a mushroom cloud.

Nodules on the ocean floor.

▓ Chapter 3 ▓
THE NODULES ARE COMING

They have been coming for over a hundred years. The first to notice them were the scientists aboard HMS *Challenger*, the magnificent three-masted square-rigger that cruised the world's oceans, setting sail on December 21, 1872, for three and a half years. Their journey had taken the scientists from Portsmouth to Lisbon, via the Bay of Biscay, past Finisterre, Gibraltar, and Madeira; far south to the icy wastes of Antarctica; to New Zealand, Fiji, and the Philippines; New Guinea, Hong Kong, and Hawaii—and from there to Tahiti.

Near the end of their epoch-making scientific endeavor—and of an infinity of oceanographic, zoological, and anthropological finds at sea and on land, of adventures, tragedies, elations, and depressions—they sank their beam trawl between Honolulu and Tahiti, "infinitely wearisome," as stated in the report. On September 11, 1875, they raised "over a peck of heavy, very compact, oval nodules" from a depth of 2,750 fathoms. On September 16, again, "from 2,350 fathoms, the trawl brought up more than half a ton of manganese nodules which filled two small casks. The great majority were small and nearly round, resembling a number of marbles with a mean diameter of three-quarters of an inch [nearly 2 cm]." Some, however, were as large as 4 inches in diameter and 2 inches thick (10 cm by 5 cm). *Challenger* scientists also noticed that the smooth upper surface was quite different from the rough and irregular lower surface.

On the way from Tahiti to Juan Fernandez islands on October 14, 1875, they again dredged a bushel of nodules, plus hundreds of whale bones and shark teeth. On November 11 a manganese nodule as big as a hen's egg was discovered.

The *Challenger's Report on Scientific Results* lists "Pumice stones surrounded by layers of the hydrated peroxide of manganese, so that they may be called manganese nodules," raised from 2,900 fathoms at Station 248 in the North Pacific. It records findings of nodules of various shapes, sizes, and composition in the Southern Ocean: at Station 160 at a depth of 2,600 fathoms; at Stations 285 and 286 in the South Pacific; and at Station 274 in the Mid Pacific, at 2,750 fathoms. They were dredged up together with whale bones, shark teeth, and such living creatures as holothurians, starfish, sponges, annelides, echinoderms, and shrimps. The red clays, volcanic glass, and radiolarian oozes that came up with them may have given the researchers some vague idea of the natural environment of these mysterious nodules. They measured them; they counted them; they sorted, sectioned, and analyzed them.

In the South Pacific they found a nodule that had accreted around a magnetic spherule of cosmic origin. It had "a coating of black magnetic iron, with a brilliant and shagreened surface." This find may have contributed to the fleeting thought that the nodules were themselves of cosmic origin.

Perhaps they had fallen into the sea as incandescent fragments following some meteoric explosion.

Not much was learned about the nodules during the following eighty years. Then, in 1952, John Mero, still an undergraduate, began his pioneering work at the University of California. "Probably the most interesting of the mineral deposits of the sea are the manganese nodules," he wrote in 1966. And, he added, "they were apparently first recognized as a potential mineral resource by MERO (1952)." Following the Second World War, partly as a consequence of the intensified military research and development conducted in the context of the war, oceanographic research and technology had made giant strides forward.

A cursory comparison of the equipment on HMS *Challenger* in 1872 with that on the *Glomar Challenger* and its successors that were to resume nodule research a hundred years later may illustrate the difference.

HMS *Challenger* was a three-masted, square-rigged wooden ship, displacing 2,300 tons, with an overall length of 60 meters. The *Glomar Challenger,* made of steel, has a length of 130 meters and displaces 10,500 tons.

For locomotion, HMS *Challenger* had to rely on wind power, which it harnessed with its 1,500 square meters of sail. It did, however, have an engine of 1,200 horsepower which was used for dredging, harbor works, and emergencies. The *Glomar Challenger* has twelve diesel-electric engines and can cruise at 12 knots.

HMS *Challenger* was manned by a commander and 20 naval officers, carried 6 scientists, and had a total complement of 240. They lived in rather overcrowded conditions. The whole of the main deck was reserved for the scientists, whose living quarters were well appointed—they had roomy cabins with bathtubs—and whose laboratories, workrooms, and storage rooms occupied most of the space. The *Glomar Challenger* carries a nautical crew of 45—modern navigation is far less labor-intensive!—and accommodates 25 scientists in magnificent air-conditioned cabins. The vessel is resplendent with recreation rooms, Lucullan kitchens, and movie theaters.

But these differences are nothing compared to the differences in scientific equipment. The navigational aids of HMS *Challenger* were modest indeed, for there had not been much progress in this field since the days of Henry the Navigator: a compass, a sextant to determine the ship's position, marine barometers for meteorological forecasting, and chronometers which helped to solve the problem of accurately determining longitudes. The chemical laboratory, with its wooden drawers and racks, looked rather medieval.

The dredge consisted of an iron frame, about 1.5 meters long, to which a bag was attached. The iron frame was dragged over the seafloor, and whatever it loosened was swept into the bag as the ship moved forward. When the seafloor was uneven, as it mostly was, the dredge did not work very well. The dredge rope broke once in a while. On one occasion, the heavy block to which it was tied flew loose and killed a cabin boy. The dredge was later replaced by a beam trawl, which proved to be more flexible and capacious.

There was a "sounding machine," consisting of a deep-sea sounding line, a reel on which this line was kept, a number of sinkers, an apparatus for detaching the sinkers when they reached the bottom, and some iron wire and disks to attach the sinkers to the disengaging apparatus during their descent; a number of india-rubber bands; and some iron gin blocks with patent sheaves for the line to reeve through. The lines were made of best Italian hemp. The whole line, 6,000 meters long, was kept on one reel. "To prevent the sounding line becoming entangled in the axle of cranks, a wooden disk, 2½ feet in diameter, was fitted at each end of the reel, and one of these discs was grooved, so that by passing a gasket over it, one of which was attached to the ship's side, and the other end held in a man's hand, the revolutions of the reel could be retarded when the impetus given by the pitching or rolling of the ship would otherwise have caused it to revolve too quickly."

There were two kinds of lead, the cup lead and the valve sounding lead—the precursors of our corers. There were a couple of sets of sieves, a tow net, a current drag, tied with a "current line" to a "watch buoy," a set of rather ingenious pressure-protected thermometers and piezometers, and a hydrometer, which measured the weight and mass of the water. An array of water bottles, some equipped with depth gauges, completed the scientific arsenal of HMS *Challenger*.

Navigational precision today is guaranteed by radio, radar, autopilot, integrated navigation and data-logging systems, gyrocompass, Doppler sonar, and satellite communication. Ships can be kept exactly in place by dynamic positioning, that is, an array of hydrophones on the seafloor communicating, through echo-sounding, the ship's exact position to a computer which automatically corrects for any movement. The navigators of HMS *Challenger* had to use their brains as computers to correct for any movement over a testing site. During dredging operations, they let their ship drift broadside to the wind.

While it took the *Challenger* crew a wearisome day, from dawn to dusk, to dredge and to haul aboard a load of ocean floor samples, today's scientists hoist a freefall grab system overboard and go about their other business. The free-fall grabber is equipped with a position-finding system for day and night operation. This instrumentarium sinks down, takes pictures, grabs samples from the ocean floor, rises, and communicates its position by radio so it can be picked up again!

There are the corers—spade corers, piston corers, box corers—to assay the ocean floor, layer by layer, with the aid of hydraulic lifting gear: cranes and derricks and winches. There are gravimeters, magnetometers, a bathysound (a probe that continuously monitors temperature, salinity, pressure, and sound velocity), and other tools—the list is far from exhausted (Figure 7). The scientists of HMS *Challenger* sank their dredges or beam trawls into the deep, deep dark and hoped for the best.

Today's scientists can see every square meter of ocean floor to be explored. With the help of various echo-sounders, air guns for seismic reflection, and a variety of "pingers," they can reconstruct an exact profile of the ocean floor. Deep-sea TV systems with multiple-shoot cameras and video recorders, underwater still-photo cameras, and stereo-photo cameras reveal and depict every detail of the hidden landscape deep down. The scientists of HMS *Challenger* had to rely on two gifted artists to re-create the ocean floor. Their impressions, revealed in drawings, watercolors, and woodcuts, display craftsmanship, realism, taste, and imagination.

The contribution that HMS *Challenger* made to the progress of oceanography—fifty tomes of new science!—was certainly no less path-breaking than the work of the *Glomar Challenger* and her more recent successors. It is amazing, looking back, to see how the ingenuity of the human brain can make up for the lack of technology, and looking forward, to imagine how technology can emerge from mind-set perimeters!

The *Challenger* scientists knew practically all we know today about the shapes, sizes, and chemical composition of the nodules.

Most nodules are small—no more than 6 to 8 centimeters, more often 2 to 3, in diameter—although a few much larger ones have been raised. The largest ever found, near the Philippines, weighed 850 kilograms. The nodules may be black or brown in external appearance, more opaque or more glossy.

The origin of the nucleus may differ. It may be organic or inorganic, of terrestrial, pelagic, or celestial origin—shark teeth, pieces of whale bone, rocks or clay or silica or, as the *Challenger* scientists knew, bits from outer space. There are also nodules with anthropogenic nuclei: shell splinters or fragments of cannonball, sunk with the memories of long-past naval battles. These

8. Sizes of areas in prospection and deposits of evaluation phases

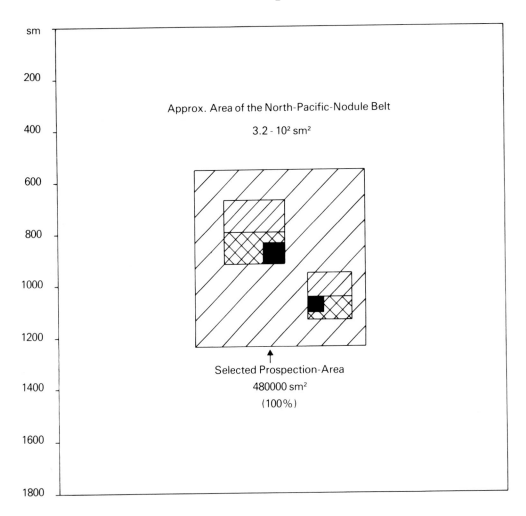

Approx. Area of the North-Pacific-Nodule Belt

3.2 · 10² sm²

Selected Prospection-Area
480000 sm²
(100%)

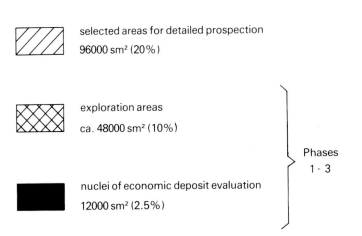

selected areas for detailed prospection
96000 sm² (20%)

exploration areas
ca. 48000 sm² (10%)

nuclei of economic deposit evaluation
12000 sm² (2.5%)

Phases
1 - 3

are nodules of a different type and are of little interest to the ocean miner. Such nodules grow rapidly: several millimeters in a few decades.

Around the nucleus, the metals accrete in concentric layers, or shells, like the skin of an onion. The manganese nodules may be round, ellipsoidal, or disklike, the shape often giving a clue to the age of the nodule. Due to a combination of environmental circumstances, "young" nodules tend to be spherical. When the spheres have reached a diameter of about 3 centimeters, they tend to accrete horizontally, assuming a more ellipsoidal shape. This is the result of a nonuniform growth rate. As they continue to accrete laterally, they eventually become discoidal in appearance. Sometimes two or three close neighbors coalesce into one polynodular shape.

All this takes millions of years. As we know today, these mysterious objects grow about one-tenth of a millimeter in a thousand years. But the methods of determining the growth rate, by measuring radioactive substances in the various "shells" within the nodule and comparing them to those present in the outermost "shell," are based on a number of uncertain premises. According to some analyses, the growth rate may be as much as ten times slower than this figure.

The *Challenger* scientists noticed that the texture of the nodules' surface was different on the lower and on the upper side. But they could not explain the difference. The lower side, in contact with the sediments, looked granular or spongy; the upper side, in contact with the water, was smooth. Could the water have polished the upper side? But the difference appeared to be more structural.

Today we are still uncertain about the reason for this difference, but at least there are theories, and very complicated ones at that. To simplify, there are quite a number of different processes, organic and inorganic, that converge in the formation of nodules. The lower part may in fact be the result of inorganic processes, the accretion of metals precipitated from ocean water to the seafloor. The upper part may be the work of living organisms, which concentrate manganese from solution in sea water into their shells, and of bacterial oxidation.

Animals may play yet another crucial role in the growth of manganese nodules. It is certain that such growth can take place only as long as the nodule remains on top of the underlying red clay sediments or radiolarian oozes. Once the nodules sink into these sediments and become buried, they cease to grow and may even disintegrate. The obvious question is, how do they manage to stay on top? The answer, already suggested in the 1950s and confirmed by research in the '60s and '70s, is: thanks to the activities of ocean floor animals. Mud-eating crawlers and burrowers plow and eat their way through the sediments and give the nodules an upward thrust.

The *Challenger* scientists compiled tables and maps listing sediments and nodules recovered at each dredging. They roughly anticipated the results of later prospecting and exploration. In some cases, however, dredging may fail to give an accurate picture of the density of nodules on the ground. Without bottom photography it is impossible to know, due to the unevenness of the terrain, whether the dredge or trawl is actually engaged on the floor or is simply passing overhead. Bottom photography thus introduced a significant refinement in nodule research. One photograph may cover up to nearly 15 square meters of a sampling area. Since as many as a thousand pictures may be taken on one single lowering of the camera, the surveyed area may cover more than 9,000 square meters.

There is nothing uniform about nodule landscapes. Some photographs show us fields of regularly spaced nodules of uniform size stretching as far as the camera takes us. Small white clouds, possibly indicating the activity of some burrowing animal, are all that breaks the regularity. In other pictures, nodules wear caps of red clay, accumulated from the rain of sediments in the area. These nodules will be stirred by the sea worms beneath, and their caps will be shaken off.

Seafloor springs carry manganese from the interior of the earth into the ocean, whose oxidizing waters precipitate the minerals. Dense concentrations of nodules have been found in the vicinity of such submarine springs.

There are swift currents below the sea, about which we as yet know very little. They lift clouds of mud off the seafloor. Sometimes they cause veritable storms. They leave the sediments in rippling waves, like the sand on wind-swept dunes; and in the valleys there are dense arrays of nodules while the crests are bare. It looks like a delicate oriental rug design.

There are nodules everywhere, except on the continental shelves and in the deep trenches. In some areas they are thinly spread; in others they are dense. Three main regions—the eastern, central, and western regions—have been singled out in the Pacific Ocean for their uniform density.

The eastern region comprises about 45 million square kilometers on both sides of the equator (parallels 0–40) and roughly between 90° and 150° longitude. The average density in the region was found to be 7.8 kilograms per square meter, with a maximum of 23 and a minimum of 5 kilograms per square meter. The central region—roughly between the same parallels but narrow around the equator and widening, like an hourglass, toward south and north—revealed even higher densities, with an average of 14.5 kilograms per square meter. The western region appears to be far less prospected, and the estimated average of 8.6 kilograms per square meter may not be accurate.

The composition of the nodules varies regionally. John Mero distinguishes four different compositional regions in the Pacific. In the "A" regions, near the coasts, nodules have a high iron content. Nodules in "B" regions, particularly near the coasts of North and South America, are high in manganese. The highest nickel and copper contents are

offered by nodules in the "C" regions, farthest removed from continental or island coasts. Finally, "D" regions, in the central part of the Pacific, are distinguished by the high cobalt content of their nodules. A high cobalt content also characterizes the nodules of the Indian Ocean.

The quantities of the nodules are truly staggering. Mero estimates the tonnage of manganese nodules on the surface of sediments of the Pacific Ocean at 1.66×10^{12} metric tons! Furthermore, assuming that they grow by about 0.1 millimeter per thousand years, this tonnage increases by 6×10^6 metric tons annually in the Pacific alone. In effect this makes nodules a renewable resource, even though it does not make them a renewable harvest. The estimates of other experts are not far from Mero's. The scientists of the Soviet Union are the most conservative. Their estimate, of 0.9×10^{11} metric tons, is about one-twentieth of Mero's. But this figure is still staggering.

Not all of the nodules can be considered a potential resource. Some may be situated in hilly regions, inaccessible to present mining technologies. Others may be too thinly scattered to make a mining operation worthwhile. In others, the metal content may be too low to warrant processing. But, as Mero pointed out in 1965, "even if only one percent of the nodules of the Pacific prove economic to mine, the reserves of many metals in the nodules will still be measured in terms of thousands of years at the present rates of free-world consumption."

If it is to satisfy the conditions set by mining economists, a potential nodule mine site must have the following properties: (1) the ocean floor must be free of major obstacles; (2) the density of the nodules must be not less than 10 kilograms per square meter; (3) the minimum metal content must be as follows:

nickel:	1.5 percent
copper:	1.3 percent
cobalt:	0.24 percent
manganese:	27.0 percent

Spade corer being lowered over the side. The
corer can be used to obtain a seabed sediment
sample of up to 45 cm in length.

Table 7: Consortia Involved in Deep Seabed Mining (September 1980)

Consortium	Company	Involvement %	Country
Kennecott	Kennecott	40	USA
	Rio Tinto Zinc	12	UK
	Consolidated Gold Fields	12	UK
	BP Minerals	12	UK
	Noranda	12	Canada
	Mitsubishi	12	Japan
Ocean Mining Associates (OMA)	US Steel	33	USA
	Union Minière	33	Belgium
	Sun Oil	33	USA
Ocean Minerals Company (OMINCO)	Lockheed	40	USA
	Standard Oil of Indiana	25	USA
	Royal Dutch Shell/Billiton	25	Netherlands/UK
	Bos Kalis Westminster	10	Netherlands
Ocean Management Inc. (OMI)	INCO	25	USA/Canada
	AMR Group	25	West Germany
	Sedco	25	USA
	DOMCO Group	25	Japan
AFERNOD	Bureau de Recherches Géologiques Minières (BRGM)	No percentages available for this group	France
	Centre National pour l'Exploitation des Océans (CNEXO)		
	Commissariat d'Energie Atomique (CEA)		
	Chantiers de France-Dunkerque		
	Société Minière de Nickel (SLN/SMN)		

SOURCE: Tony Marjoram et al., "Manganese Nodules and Marine Technology," p. 48.

The site must yield approximately 3 million dry metric tons of nodules a year, and the life expectancy of the mine site must be twenty to twenty-five years.

Much as Mero has been criticized for overoptimism, there is not one expert contributing to the voluminous literature on the nascent nodule mining industry who would question that 1 percent of Mero's estimated resource would meet these criteria. This means a reserve of thousands of years of these metals which are so crucial for industrial development. A new age of mining has indeed begun.

Let us now follow, in our minds, a mining project as it might develop over a twenty-five-year period, beginning in the year 1990.

The company undertaking the project would be one of the multinational consortia that have been formed over the past ten or fifteen years to spread risks and to share research and development costs for an industry whose initial difficulties rival those encountered in outer space. In 1984 there are five such international consortia in existence, including companies from the USA, Canada, the Federal Republic of Germany, France, Belgium, the Netherlands, the United Kingdom, Italy, and Japan (Table 7). The Soviet Union is heavily engaged in its own research and development in deep-sea mining.

During most of the project life, our imaginary consortium will work in close association with the newly created United Nations International Seabed Authority, established by the Convention on the Law of the Sea that was adopted by the Third United Nations Conference on the Law of the Sea in 1982. This Authority is responsible for the management of mineral exploration and exploitation on the deep seabed.

There are, roughly speaking, seven distinct though overlapping phases involved in the twenty-five-year project: research and development, prospecting, exploration, mining, transportation, processing, and marketing.

The first phase involves not only the industrial companies but also a number of universities and technological institutions, government departments, and international institutions. It is a broadly interdisciplinary effort, ranging from marine geology and geophysics to mining engineering, and covering chemistry, mineralogy, metallurgy, biology, paleontology, acoustics, photography, satellite communication, systems engineering, nautical engineering, and navigation.

Since all the consortia have already successfully concluded this first phase—in most cases with a mining test effectively proving the technical feasibility of the undertaking—we need not strain our imagination. We may simply record what has already happened.

Perhaps the most exciting event of this kind was the *SEDCO* mining test, completed in 1978, which was the first time that manganese nodules were mined continuously and in large quantities. This was achieved by Ocean Management, Inc., a group of American, Canadian, Japanese, and West German consortia, most of them in turn being composed of several national companies. The ship on which all efforts converged was the converted pilot mining ship *SEDCO 445*, owned and operated by the American partner of the same name. Originally the *SEDCO* was an oil-drilling ship. It displaces 17,150 tons, is 135 meters long, and is equipped with a diesel electric engine of 9,000 horsepower, twin screws propulsion, eleven lateral thrusters, and a computerized dynamic positioning system. It is interesting, though not surprising, to note how much seabed mining technology is indebted to offshore oil-drilling technology. This may help explain the heavy involvement of the oil industry in this new mining sector. This involvement may also be motivated by the possibility—perhaps an unlikely one—that nodule exploration and the development of nodule technology could result in the discovery of large oil fields on the deep seabed.

The main changes that had to be made to the *SEDCO* to prepare it for its new mission related to the installation of a Hydra rig mast, the power supply for the mining operation, the installation of air compressors to activate the air-lift system, and certain hull modifications to make room for nodule storage.

The assemblage of the mining and lifting system was a truly cooperative effort among the companies of four nations on three continents. The design and engineering of the hydraulic unit was the main Japanese (DOMCO) contribution. The pipe string was designed by Canada's INCO and produced in Germany by Mannesmann. Design, fabrication, and pre–pilot mining test work on the hydraulic pumps and accessories was the responsibility of AMR in Germany. All these components were brought to the Bethlehem Steel shipyard in Beaumont, Texas. Preassembled complete vans containing installed equipment were mounted directly onto the ship. The whole transformation was completed in forty days!

The test got under way step by step. Some component tests were made dockside. Two short cruises followed, the first off the coast of Texas, the next all the way to Hawaii. By that time the multinational crew had become accustomed to one another and to the sophisticated new equipment on their odd-looking vessel.

The Hydra rig is as peculiar as its name. Were it "hydrorig," it would mean a "water rig"; but it is "Hydra rig." It so happens that the scientists on HMS *Challenger* had a "Hydra sounding machine . . . so called from its having been made by the blacksmith of H.M.S. 'Hydra,' as an improvement on Brooke's rod, the American invention," as the *Challenger* report states. Could the memory of this modest instrument have been invoked with the naming of this enormous and sophisticated construction?

The Hydra rig is essential for the deployment and retrieval of the 5-kilometer-long dredging pipe. The assemblage of the roughly 400 parts and special sections over the mine site requires an enormous amount of precision on the part of the crew and steadiness on the part of the rig, which has to be kept in an exactly vertical position even when the ship rolls and pitches. A solution to this problem was found in a gyro-controlled system, activating four hydraulic cylinders at the base of the mast.

Then the *SEDCO* took off to its selected site in the Mid Pacific. The weather was beautiful and the sea calm throughout, thanks to good fortune combined with meteorological foresight.

The *SEDCO* stops and activates its dynamic positioning system. Hydrophones are lowered to the seafloor, 5 kilometers below. Though the site has been carefully explored before, free-fall grab samplers and photographic equipment are lowered overboard.

Current meters, indicating directions and long- and short-term variations of deep-sea currents, are anchored to the seabed. Thermometers and water bottles are lowered. Measuring results are computerized. When all is clear, the main operation begins.

The collector is sitting in the "moon pool," the opening through which the pipe string is lowered into the ocean. The collector is constructed so as to ride on the surface of the ocean floor without sinking too deeply into the sediments. During the prepilot tests, a collector or photo-sledge became buried several times in the red clay and capsized as it was dragged along.

The collector must gather as high a proportion of the nodules as possible and reject oversized objects. It must separate nodules from sediments and eliminate as much of the fine sediment as possible right on the ground. Finally, it must feed the material to the opening of the lift system. A variety of collector systems had been experimented with prior to the pilot test. One hydraulically powered and one mechanically powered system were continuously monitored by underwater real-time television and other devices. Power to the collector and for data transfer was provided by several thick high-power cables running from the ship to the seafloor.

We are standing near the base of the Hydra rig. The first piece of pipe string is being attached to the collector. The first twenty to thirty sections are made of rubber hose, so as to ensure flexibility and allow the collector to move over minor irregularities on the seafloor. Steel pipe and special sections follow. About 12 meters in length, the steel pipe sections are similar in appearance to oil-field casing. They are automatically lifted from their storage place on deck and placed vertically in the Hydra rig. Three men fasten the joints between sections with wrenches. They work rapidly, with the precision of machines. There are 400 sections. The special sections carry various instrumentation and control packages. An instrument platform is attached and lowered to 2,000 meters. It comprises a TV camera, strobe lights, spotlights, and housings with electronic control units. All these components must be air-pressure-protected to work effectively at a depth of 5,000 meters.

During some of the tests, submerged hydraulic pumps were installed in the pipe string; during others, three air compressors provided pressurized air for an air-lift system. The compressed air is conducted through a tube running outside the pipe string and injected into the pipe at about 2,000 meters depth. As the air expands it creates an upward flow and activates the air-lift. Both systems worked equally well.

It takes about six hours of intense work to assemble this huge apparatus. Then comes the climax. The collector is activated. We watch what happens from the TV studio on board. The collector moves over the ground at a brisk walking speed of about 6 kilometers per hour, filling with nodules, pushing its load toward the lift pipe. The pumps are activated. The fifteen minutes it takes the first nodules to travel the 5 kilometers of the pipe seem endless—the calm before the storm. Then they arrive. The nodules are coming so fast it is unbelievable. It looks as though the coal delivery man has gone insane, flooding our basement with an uninterrupted mass. It looks as though the sorcerer's apprentice has again unleashed uncontrollable forces. It looks like a natural disaster.

The speed at which the nodules are disgorged on board is, however, well calculated. It must be high. To make mining economical, the ship must mine at least 3 million tons a year. Allowing for 320 working days—there will be some days when not even the gyro-controlled system can keep the Hydra rig vertical in the storm-lashed seas and other days when the ship is undergoing repairs—SEDCO must mine nearly 10,000 tons a day! SEDCO proved that it can be done. After half a day, the pumps are stopped.

Three times the SEDCO 445 ventured forth, to different sites, experimenting with air-lift and hydraulic pumps. Then she returned to Hawaii, and from there to Texas. In Beaumont, on the same dock where she

was armed as a pioneer nodule miner, she was reconverted into an ordinary oil-drilling vessel. Since July 1978, the SEDCO 445 has lived a more mundane life and there is nothing extraordinary to report about her.

This particular phase of research and development lasted three and a half years. The R&D phase is partly preceded by and partly overlaps the second phase, that of prospecting. Prospecting has gone on since the early 1970s. It will continue as part of every new mining project.

In the future, prospecting may take place only under a license issued by the International Seabed Authority. The Authority will encourage prospecting, provided applicants undertake to comply with rules and regulations concerning the protection of the marine environment and some other basic rules of the road.

Prospecting means a widely spaced, mostly linear, generic survey of a relatively large area. The area may cover as much as half a million square nautical miles, running through barren plain interrupted by mountain ranges, stretches disturbed by soil slides, seamounts or steep slopes of basaltic material, lava streams, or block fields. Hills may be 16 kilometers long and up to 5 kilometers wide. All this has to be carefully mapped by TV profiling or side-scan sonar.

The way in which the nodules are arranged on the seabed does not make life easy for the mining consortia. It appears that there are no continuous accessible deposits larger than about 100 square kilometers. The metal contents of the nodules also seem to vary over very short distances, from one 10-square-kilometer patch to the next. Tough luck—or is it nature—appears to have arranged it so that just where the nodules are densest, their quality is lowest. Where they are more sparsely distributed, the metal grade is higher. So much so that prospectors and explorers have put it into the form of an equation:

$$\frac{\text{population density} \times \text{metal content}}{\text{unit area}} = \pm \text{ constant}$$

("metal content" meaning nickel, copper, and cobalt). The fortune of prospecting hinges on the ±.

The essential goal of the prospecting phase is to narrow down the prospecting area for the next phase, exploration. The total area of the North Pacific nodule belt is estimated to cover 3.2 million square nautical miles (11 million sq km). A prospecting area of about 500,000 square nautical miles (1.6 million sq km) is first staked out. Within this, two more or less promising areas, each about 10 percent of the total, are singled out for more detailed prospection. With a total area of 100,000 square nautical miles (320,000 sq km), the area selected for detailed investigation is equivalent to, say, eight times the surface area of the Netherlands.

Echo-sounders of various types are operated. They record the stratification of the upper 50 meters of sediment. The mapping of the seafloor, with soundings taken at decreasing distances, requires special navigation systems. These, again, consist mostly of echo-sounders, either on board or towed near the ocean floor, to indicate any morphological obstacle.

Sonar tools, which emit periodic impulses of a fixed frequency, transmit to the ship the exact distance between the towed equipment and the ocean floor. They carry special sensors to register pressure, temperature, and salinity.

Another basic prospecting tool is the seismic air gun. The high-energy blast generated by the gun penetrates the water column and the sediments all the way down to the basaltic rock bottom. Hydrophone chains, which are towed behind the ship, transmit the echoes traveling with different sound velocities through various strata and thus provide information about sediment stratification. They also indicate the presence of rock outcrops, obstacles to future mining.

For the layman the most impressive information comes from the optical instruments, TV systems and still camera, that make the new world comprehensible to our senses. It is anticipated that TV scanning

may be increasingly replaced by laser scanning, which gives the observer the impression that he is really walking among the nodules in their mysterious environment.

The prospecting phase and the exploration phase obviously overlap. Exploration is essentially prospecting in considerably more detail. The three essentials of exploration, as formulated by Dr. Rainer Fellerer, an expert of the German mining firm Preussag AG, are:

1. acquisition of data about the ore and its substratum;
2. mapping of the ocean floor, followed by the compilation of deposit maps; and
3. development and handling of exploration equipment for greatest efficiency as well as improving the strategies for exploration.

These three main functions affect one another. Oceanological and meteorological data have to be added.

The difference between prospecting and exploration is that the area will have been narrowed down to less than 50,000 square nautical miles (160,000 sq km) or, rather, to two distinct areas, each about half that size (Figures 8 and 9). Air gun seismic echo-sounding, sampling, TV profiling, with wire-bound or free-fall instruments, are intensified. If, during the prospecting phase, sample points have been separated by more than 160 kilometers (more than ten hours' sailing time), the exploration phase narrows this distance to about 2 kilometers. About twenty tests can thus be made daily. Tests continue in each of the exploration areas until a nucleus is identified in which the nodules are distributed evenly enough to permit an economic evaluation. This may cover 12,000 square nautical miles (at 38,000 square kilometers still about the size of the Netherlands!), or just about 2.5 percent of the area originally prospected. This becomes the site of a feasibility study which forms the basis for a detailed plan of work for the expected lifetime of the mine site.

While prospecting is free—under the

9. Exploration phases for final evaluation of deposits

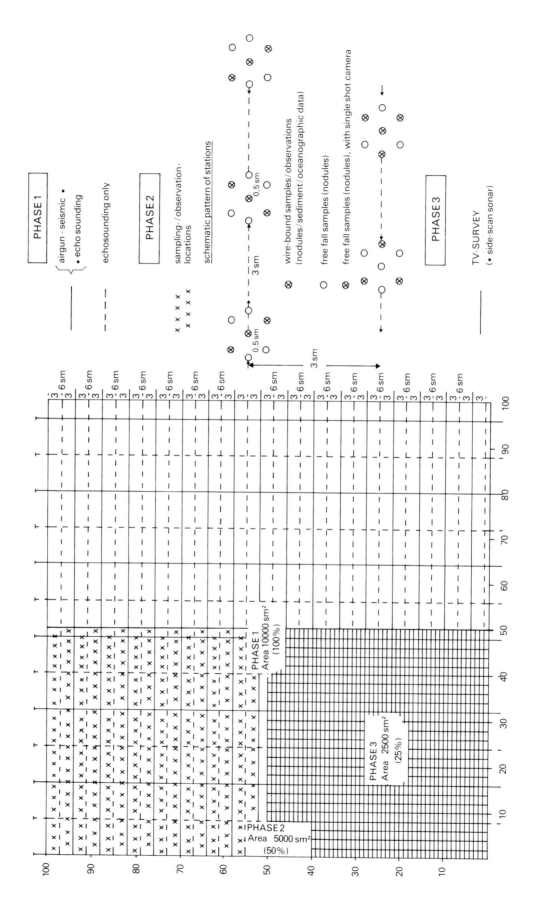

Law of the Sea Convention as adopted, no taxes need be paid to the International Seabed Authority—exploration takes place only under some form of association with the Authority, be it in the form of a contract or of a joint venture. In the case of a contract, elaborate controls and payment schedules are contained in the Law of the Sea Convention. Whether contract or joint venture, however, the detailed plan of work must in any case be approved by the technical and deliberative bodies of the Authority.

The total time for the economic evaluation, spread over forty-one cruises during three years, may have run up to a thousand days at sea, plus land-based logistic support and laboratory work. Between research and development, prospecting, and exploration, seven years may have passed.

We may be near the year 2000. Now the actual mining phase begins. The nodules are coming on stream: perhaps a million tons during the first year, then at a rate of 3 million tons per annum.

The actual mining operation will look much like the *SEDCO* pilot mining test described above, although other technologies may also be used. One well-known technology, developed and tested by the Japanese, is the so-called continuous line bucket system (CLB), in which a large number of buckets are dragged over the ocean floor, picking up nodules and sediments as they go. The sediments escape through holes in the buckets during the ascent to the ship. The operation of the 10,000- to 12,000-meter-long continuous line has caused certain obvious difficulties, which the Japanese have sought to overcome by rotating the line over two ships positioned some distance apart, rather than a single ship. But this further increases the length of the line. As things now stand, it does not look as though the CLB system will become commercially viable. The large quantities of nodules that would have to be mined to make a venture commercially feasible would require the operation of a dozen or so CLB systems, and this gives rise to problems which may defeat even the Japanese.

However, there are experts who have more confidence in the CLB system than in other systems that are even more complicated. A simple system has obvious advantages and might be of interest to developing countries interested in ocean mining.

Another somewhat futuristic design, already on the drawing board, has been developed by the French. Here nodules are raised, not in a pipe nor in buckets, but in free-plunging mining shuttles. Each shuttle—and there may be hundreds involved in one operation—is equipped with a television camera and lights, remote controlled and steered from above. Each one plunges down to the bottom independently, scoops up its nodules, and returns to the mother ship.

Whatever the lifting system adopted, the mining ships are now part of a system that includes a number of ore carriers, which transport the nodules to the mainland. The mainland port may be several thousand kilometers away, in a location where conditions facilitate the siting of a nodule processing plant.

Ore carriers can hold a load of 60,000 to 80,000 tons, the product of about one week of mining. The mining ship itself usually has storage space for just about that quantity, so once a week an empty carrier will be needed on station. The nodules are transferred from the mining ship to the carrier through a slurry pipe. The number of carriers required obviously depends on the distance between the port and the mining operation and on the carrier's capacity. A few large carriers are less costly than more numerous smaller ones. The size of the carrier, however, is limited by the capacity of the port serving it and by other constraints encountered in the course of the journey (straits, shallows, etc.). It is all part of very complex logistics.

Mining, transportation, and processing phases are obviously concurrent. They also overlap with the exploration phase, which continues as long as mining goes on. Mining, just like exploration, is carried out under contract to the Authority or in joint venture with it. Transportation and processing fall

10. The Atlantis II Deep

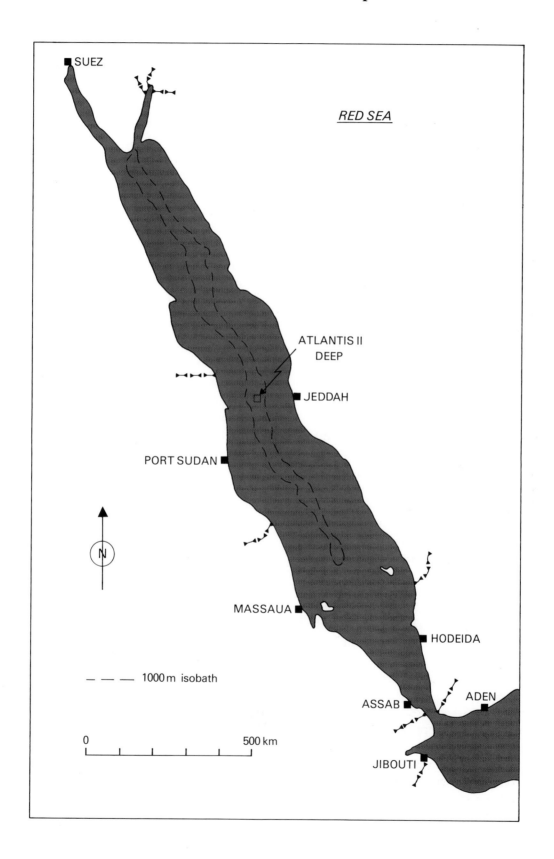

RED SEA

SUEZ

ATLANTIS II
DEEP

JEDDAH

PORT SUDAN

N

MASSAUA

HODEIDA

— — — 1000 m isobath

ASSAB   ADEN

0   500 km

JIBOUTI

outside the jurisdiction of the Authority and are carried out under national responsibility. The Authority itself may, however, carry out integrated mining projects, including transportation, processing, and marketing, and may do so in joint venture with companies or states.

From the seabed, the project has now moved to the water surface. The ore carrier is a traditional ship, integrated in a global network of navigational and meteorological aids, including radio, radar, land-based, sea-based, and satellite-based support. These technologies have made gigantic strides during the past twenty years. Major improvements in safety, speed, and efficiency have been achieved, and further improvements loom on the horizon.

One could imagine a systems breakthrough with the further development of very large submarines. Earlier we took note of the possibility, and the advantages, of separating the gathering from the lifting process in the mining system itself. Here we might—just thinking aloud and in an admittedly somewhat daring fashion—envisage the possibility of eliminating the immensely delicate and costly lifting phase altogether by gathering on the seafloor and loading directly onto huge submarine ore carriers which would deliver the nodules directly to the port. A 60,000-ton deadweight submarine is quite within the realm of the possible. Loading and shipping would go on in the calm deep, independent of weather hazards on the surface, with enormous savings in energy and a reduction of hazards. The impact on the environment would also be notably decreased. John Craven's "rule" would again ring true: deeper is cheaper.

The next phase of the integrated mining project, the processing phase, moves us out of Neptune's realm to terra firma. At least for the foreseeable future, processing will take place on shore, although the problems it entails are such that eventually this phase may be moved back to sea. But we want to envisage the process such as it now appears to be taking shape.

The ore carrier has docked in the harbor, which might be in Hawaii, on the west coast of the USA, or in one of the Latin American countries; or it might be on Fiji or another one of the Pacific islands, or on the Pacific coast of Asia—anywhere between 500 and 3,000 nautical miles from the mining site. The choice of the processing site, and the port to serve it, will depend on a number of factors including energy supply, availability of cooling water, and environmental considerations. The port facilities include a slurry pipeline into which the nodules will be fed and transported to the processing plant, let us say 8 kilometers away from the harbor.

The processing of the nodules, that is, the extraction of their valuable metal content and the disposal of the remainder, has been compared to the process of food ingestion and digestion by a living organism. First the food is crushed, being chewed by the teeth. Similarly, the nodules are first crushed and then ground. Just as the crushed food is then moved into the stomach where gastric juices set upon it for "processing," the crushed nodules are moved on to a fluid-bed furnace where the metal oxides contained in the nodule powder are reduced. The reduced ore is then fed into a series of mixing vessels and thickeners. Air is injected into the vessels to oxidize the metals into soluble ammonia complexes. This liquid is then passed through a sequence of liquidation exchange columns to separate the nickel, copper, and cobalt. These separated metals are forwarded to special tanks where the pure metals are recovered. That corresponds to the absorption of the valuable food substances which nourish the body. The indigestible food parts are eliminated through the intestinal and ureteric system. Similarly, the leach solution, stripped of the valuable metals, is recycled and the tailings from the final thickener are transported to a steam stripping tower where the "gastric juices"—ammonia and carbon dioxide—are recovered.

There are other metallurgical processes that could be applied to the extraction of the metals. Hydrometallurgical techniques appear to have certain advantages. The choice of process will depend on local circumstances; some countries already have metallurgical plants and technologies that could be adapted to nodule processing.

The energy requirements vary according to the process adopted. In all cases, however, they are considerable, in terms of hydrocarbons and electricity needed for the transport of the slurry, the crushing and drying, the production of steam needed for the recovery of ammonia from the tailings, and cooling. The power generated by a full-size Ocean Thermal Energy Conversion (OTEC) plant would be adequate to do the job (for a description of OTEC systems, see Chapter 5). Energy costs account for about 30 percent of the total processing cost. Processing, in turn, is the most costly phase of the whole mining undertaking, accounting for almost 70 percent of the capital costs and about 64 percent of the operating costs of an integrated mining project, the total cost of which may run around several billion dollars.

Whatever the technology applied, the final stage will consist of feeding the tailings into another slurry pipe—the end of the intestinal tract—and transporting them to the processing plant's waste disposal site. This may be some distance away, and it raises a major problem.

The useful metal content of the nodules, it will be recalled, is very small. If iron and manganese are not to be processed for reasons of economy, as some consortia intend, only 2.5 percent of the dry nodule weight is utilized. This means that 97.5 percent goes into the tailings and must be disposed of. If 3 million tons are mined annually, this represents about 2,925,000 tons of waste material a year!

It has been estimated that a waste disposal area of 99 acres will be required for every year in which 3 million tons of nodules are processed. That means 2,475 acres of wasteland covered with poisonous rubble by the year 2015. This certainly is a major environmental problem. True, if manganese were

also to be processed, the wasteland could be reduced by a factor of 10. If other metals, including iron or trace metals like molybdenum, were to be processed, there could be a further reduction. The "wastes" could be stored for future recovery. But the problem remains substantial. There must be more imaginative ways of dealing with it. Suppose the leaching chemicals could be removed from the tailings more effectively; could these tailings not be utilized as building materials, for landfills, or pressed into concrete?

Unless and until such applications are invented and the spin-offs for industrial diversification are increased, the social and environmental costs of a nodule processing plant appear rather forbidding. Industrialized countries seem to be set on banning them from their shores. Developing countries would be well advised to calculate carefully the pros and cons.

The alternative would be to move them out to sea, onto a floating factory right next to the mine site. This would drastically reduce transportation costs. It would also reduce energy costs: energy could be generated from the oceans themselves through Ocean Thermal Energy Conversion systems, particularly applicable in the tropical seas where nodule mining will take place, since the difference between the warm upper layers and the cold bottom waters is greatest in these regions. The Mini-OTEC, a pilot plant currently operating remarkably successfully in the waters of Hawaii, points in this direction. Financially supported by the companies interested in mining and processing, the Mini-OTEC may indeed presage bigger and better things to come.

Processing at sea would also ensure unlimited supplies of cooling water. And it would eliminate the tremendous waste disposal problem on land.

However, it would also create other problems. It would aggravate the impact of ocean mining on the marine environment. Even without processing at sea, this impact may be quite serious and requires further study and new approaches and solutions.

There can be no doubt that even during the prospecting and exploration phases, seismic profiling may kill fish in the immediate vicinity of the blast, even if in negligible quantities. During the mining phase, the damage is multiple and intense. German scientist Ludwig Karbe of Hamburg University concludes:

> There can be no doubt that the benthic community on the sea floor will be destroyed by the collector over a wide area. Based on the findings of DOMES site C, the daily mortality per mining unit was calculated to be about 240 million specimen of macro- and meso-fauna corresponding to a biomass of 783 kg. The consequences of this mortality on the total community cannot be predicted. It is to be expected that part of the bottom will remain unaffected by the collector and that recolonization will take place. However, as deep sea benthic productivity is usually slow and as reproduction may take longer than in other zones of the world's oceans, it is obvious that alterations in community structure and biomass will be a consequence of these operations.

The direct effects of the collector scraping on the seafloor are compounded by the indirect effects of increased turbidity in the water column. Sediments are stirred up far and wide. As the collector moves along the ground, it leaves behind it a trail, or "plume," of turbidity. A second plume is generated by the discharge of sediments after the nodules reach the ship. The turbidity, Karbe points out, will have harmful effects on filter-feeding bottom organisms that are found in the nodule region, such as sponges, crinoids, asteroids, bivalves, and tunicates.

The turbidity generated in the upper layers of water by sediment discharges from the ship obstructs the penetration of light. The so-called euphotic layer of the water, the layer penetrated by sunlight, normally about 100 meters deep, is reduced to 50 meters. This decreases primary phytoplankton pro-

duction by about 50 percent, which in turn has an effect on the entire food chain. By the time the ship leaves, it has changed the physical conditions of the habitat, which may be an additional cause for changes in species composition.

If one adds the effects of processing to those of mining, the damage is multiplied by a factor of several magnitudes. One can imagine the plume in the wake of a continuous discharge of millions of tons of tailings. And to this vastly increased physical damage one has still to add the chemical damage from the discharge of poisonous leaching substances. We might create a dead sea in the middle of the ocean, with effects on the rest of the ocean system we cannot predict.

What is to be done?

Some of the industrial firms themselves are wary, and this is much to their credit. The international community has begun to formulate certain rules of international law to protect the marine environment from any harmful effects of seabed mining. The Convention on the new Law of the Sea states that necessary measures must be taken "to ensure effective protection of the marine environment from harmful effects which may arise" from ocean mining. It enjoins the Authority to "adopt rules, regulations and procedures for the prevention of pollution and contamination and other hazards to the marine environment . . . and of interference with the ecological balance of the marine environment, particular attention being paid to the need for protection from the consequences of such activities as drilling, dredging, excavation, disposal of waste, construction and operation or maintenance of installations, pipelines and other activities related to such activities." Rules and regulations are also to be drawn up "to secure effective protection of the marine environment from harmful effects directly resulting from . . . shipboard processing immediately above a mine site of minerals derived from the mine site, taking into account the extent to which such harmful effects may directly result from drilling, dredging, coring and excavation as well as disposal, dumping, and discharge into the marine environment of sediments, wastes or other effluents."

Finally, the Authority's executive organ, the Council, is empowered to "disapprove areas for exploitation . . . in cases where substantial evidence indicates the risk of serious harm to the marine environment." (In an earlier version, the text specified "serious harm to a unique environment," which presumably would have included the life-teeming "thermal oases" mentioned in the opening pages of this book.)

All this is encouraging. It is no more, however, than the statement of a problem: a challenge. The response must come from technological and economic developments.

Ideally, one would imagine that the resource exploration phase should be concurrent with a detailed ecological exploration phase. Existing marine life should be recolonized before the mining begins and the collector initiates its baneful activity. The discharge of sediments should be completed, as far as possible, on the seafloor itself, thus eliminating the plume from shipboard and the ensuing turbidity in the upper water column.

In any case, one should aim at a reduction in the number of phases in the mining process: either the elimination of the lifting process by loading directly onto submarines and processing on land, or the elimination of the transport of the nodules by processing at sea. The elimination of stages will decrease the amount of pollution; it will also reduce the cost of the project.

Processing, whether on land or at sea, will have to be developed as a closed system, with the complete recycling of all chemical substances, linked to a factory system utilizing the tailings for production. Such factory systems could be constructed on artificial islands which are mobile, self-propelling, and can follow the mining ship from mine site to mine site. If there remains an irreducible core of waste, this should be deposited in a morphologically restricted deep, perhaps one of the deep ocean trenches. Perfection, however, is not of this world. Some damage will be done. It may be of some consolation that it will be less than would be done by comparable mining operations on land.

Our imaginary mining project has now moved through six of its seven stages: research and development, prospecting, exploration, mining, transportation, and processing. Ten years may have passed. We are moving toward the final stage: marketing. Now the project begins to pay.

We need to consider briefly three aspects of this final phase: the end use of the metals, the impact of ocean mining on the world economy, and its consequences for the structure of international relations.

About 40 percent of world nickel production goes into the making of stainless steel. Stainless steel sheet metal is used in the chemical industry, in automobiles, and in a great variety of consumer goods. Another major proportion of nickel production (16 percent) is used for electroplating, most of it in the automobile industry. Yet another part (about 12 percent) is consumed in the form of high-nickel heat-resistant super-alloys by the chemical and petrochemical industries, in the making of industrial furnaces, and in the aviation industry. Nickel (about 10 percent of total production) is used in the production of structural alloy steels for oil and gas pipelines and in the construction of aircraft and other vehicles. Nickel is also vital for the production of military equipment and related high technologies, such as aerospace, aeronautics, nuclear, desalination, pollution control, and some marine technologies.

The nickel used in the production of stainless steel and other alloys can be replaced, more or less satisfactorily, by other metals, for instance by chromium, molybdenum, vanadium, columbium, or cobalt. An overproduction of cobalt and a resulting drop in cobalt prices may thus also affect the nickel market. About 20 to 30 percent of nickel production comes from scrap; that is, nickel is to a large extent subject to recycling. Nickel is tough and resistant to heat and corrosion.

Copper also has a high resistance to corrosion. It is moreover a good conductor of heat and electricity and is extremely malleable. Hence its large-scale use—about 50 percent of total production—in electrical and electronic products, such as cables, wires, motors, and generators. Anyone who has seen the copper roofs, with their lovely green patina, on churches, belfries, courthouses, parliaments, or other public buildings knows that copper is used extensively in the building industry on account of both its beauty and its resistance to corrosion. Copper is also used in the automobile, shipbuilding, and railroad construction industries. A number of smaller uses, such as copper pots and pans and the use of copper in bronze in sculpture and other decorative arts, completes the picture.

Copper, we recalled earlier, was the base of a whole civilization which lasted for millennia. Today copper faces sharp competition from, among others, aluminum, plastics, stainless steel, and optical fibers. Thus, if stainless steel production should rise due to a drop in the costs of nickel production, the copper market would be affected. About 50 percent of total copper consumption is accounted for by recycling.

Cobalt, like nickel and copper, has a high resistance to heat. It is tough, and in addition has magnetic properties, making it an essential component of permanent magnets. It is a highly strategic metal, used in aircraft engines and turbines. Its use in medicine, especially in cancer treatment, is well known. In many applications, cobalt and nickel are interchangeable. Given the much higher price of cobalt, industrial firms have so far tended to decrease the use of cobalt and to increase the use of nickel. If, with nodule production coming on stream, the price of cobalt drops sharply, this will undoubtedly bite into the nickel market. Recycling plays a very minor role in cobalt production.

Manganese is used mainly as a chemical agent to desulphurize and deoxidize steel and in the production of dry-cell batteries. It is also used as a toughening and hardening alloy in steel production. It is a strategic metal, especially in the USA.

Trade in these four major metals plays an important role in the relations between the industrialized world and the developing countries of Africa, Asia, and Latin America. Consumption is heavily concentrated in the industrialized countries, which in 1977 consumed as much as 94 percent of the world's nickel production and almost 90 percent of the world's copper. While there are no reliable data available for the consumption of cobalt and manganese, it is certain that these metals are also overwhelmingly consumed by the factories of the industrialized countries.

Production is far more diversified than consumption. Canada, the USSR, and Australia, among the developed countries, are major producers of nickel. Developing countries (in particular New Caledonia, Cuba, and the Philippines) account for 33.5 percent of world production.

The production of copper is almost evenly divided between industrialized and developing countries, the main producers being the USA (17 percent), USSR (14.2 percent), Canada (9.7 percent), and, within the Third World, Chile (13.2 percent), Zambia (8.2 percent), and Zaire (6 percent). The developing countries' collective share is 44 percent. Cobalt, in contrast, is overwhelmingly produced by developing countries (66.9 percent). The developing countries' collective share in manganese production is 31.7 percent; by far the most important producers are the USSR and the Republic of South Africa.

The difference between industrialized and developing-country producers is, of course, that the economies of the industrialized countries are far more diversified than those of the developing countries. Third World countries typically depend on the production and export of one or two commodities, destined mostly for Western countries, often those that in the past were their colonial overlords. The same companies that exploited these resources in the colonies frequently continue to do so under the new regime of political, but not economic, sovereignty.

While the benefits derived by the former colonies from the exploitation of their resources by their former colonial overlords are not always what they were hoped to be, any reduction that might result from the development of alternative resources, such as the nodules, would certainly affect their economies; just how much nodule mining could eventually cut into this postcolonial extraction economy is at present extremely difficult to say. One of the aims of the nodule miners of the industrialized countries is undoubtedly to reduce their dependence on politically unstable environments for strategically important metals and minerals. Increased resource independence for industrialized countries, however, entails the danger of increased marginalization for developing countries.

The United Nations Conference on Trade and Development (UNCTAD) has estimated possible losses in foreign exchange earnings of developing countries to be as high as $2.3 billion for copper by the year 2000, $104 million for manganese, $1.11 billion for cobalt, and $3.86 billion for nickel. The estimates are, however, based upon very hypothetical assumptions.

The imponderables are indeed many: economic recession or depression; a decrease in demand; new discoveries on land; substitutions; new uses for the metals in question; war or peace. An array of economic, technological, social, and political factors may impact on the decision on whether, when, and how much to mine from the seabed. All we can say today is that if and when seabed mining takes place, it will have one of two consequences for the developing countries that produce the same metals on land, and for the relations between these and the industrialized countries: If the industrialized countries proceed unilaterally, the net effect will be negative. Seabed mining will contrib-

ute to the marginalization of the developing countries, and thereby to increased instability, unrest, and tension. If, on the other hand, seabed mining is carried out as provided for by the Convention on the Law of the Sea, through an International Seabed Authority, then the results may be quite different. In this case, ocean mining would be a common effort to utilize the common heritage of mankind for the benefit of mankind as a whole. If developing countries, through the International Seabed Authority, fully participate in the new industry, they will not necessarily lose export earnings. They will export seabed minerals while conserving their own land-based resources. By joining the industrialized countries in the management of seabed resources, the developing countries will benefit from the transfer of technology and the acquisition of management skills: new tools for development strategy. Through international cooperation, they can take part in the new phase of the industrial revolution, skipping phases, catching up. At last they will be able to diversify their economies, to break the grip of a postcolonial extraction economy, and to establish economic sovereignty as an essential complement to political sovereignty.

It is not the financial value of the nodules and their metals and minerals that would account for such miracles. It is the new mode of international cooperation based on the principles of common heritage and collective economic security that would be a catalyst for change. The Seabed Authority would be only the first in a series of much-needed public international resource-management institutions.

We shall return to this in the final chapter.

11. General view of mud-mining system

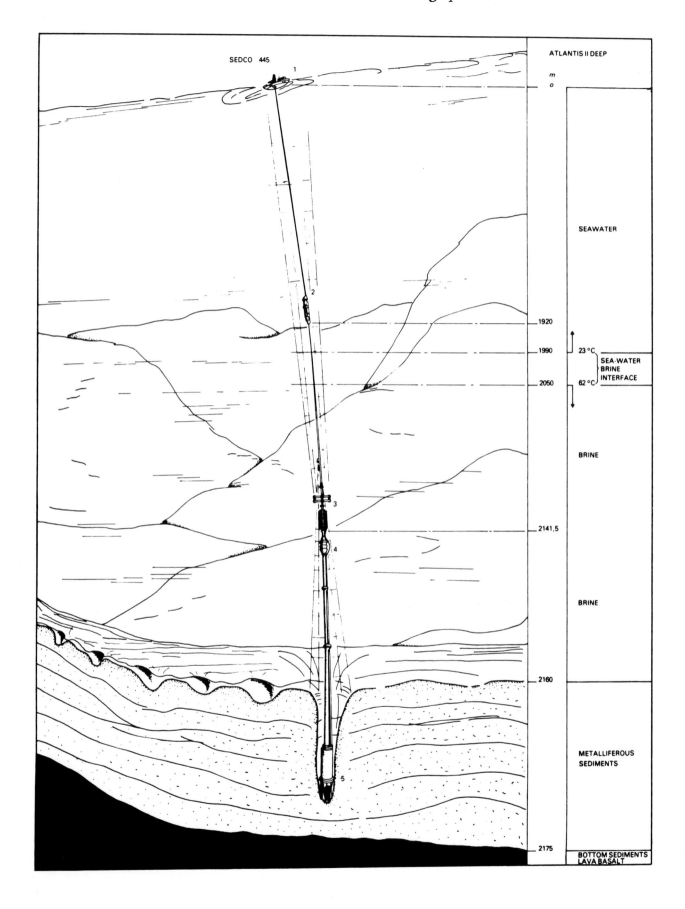

▓ Chapter 4 ▓
THE RICHES OF THE RED SEA

It was more or less a chance discovery. Since the opening of the Suez Canal, the Red Sea had been the main highway leading from the Atlantic/Mediterranean ocean system to the Indian/Pacific. During the 1960s it so happened that research vessels from many countries traveled that road to join the International Indian Ocean Expedition. To make good use of ship time, they conducted routine tests as they steamed along: The *Atlantis* (1963), *Atlantis II* (1963, 1965), *Discovery* (1963, 1964, 1967), *Oceanographer* (1967), *Meteor* (1964, 1965), *Academician Vavilov* (1966), and *Chain* (1966).

That the Red Sea had some peculiarities, such as abnormal variations in salinity and temperature, had been known since the Swedish *Albatross* expedition of 1948, but nobody had paid much attention to it. With the technologies now at the disposal of this new generation of research ships, the source of these abnormal variations was identified in the "Deeps," some of which now bear the names of the ships that discovered them. Seventeen "Deeps" were discovered along a rift valley running through the middle of the Red Sea, the deepest one, the Suakin Deep, reaching a depth of 2,850 meters. Some of the deeps were filled with hot brines with a salinity of up to 125 parts per thousand and a temperature of almost 62°C. And at the bottom of the brines there were layers of muds, and the muds turned out to contain valuable metals.

The richest of the Deeps is the Atlantis II Deep, where the sediments occur at a depth of about 2,180 meters, covering a surface of about 60 square kilometers. According to a rough estimate made by the scientists of *Atlantis II,* these muds contain about 2.5 million tons of zinc, half a million tons of copper, and about 9,000 tons of silver worth $6.7 billion at 1976 prices. In addition, they contain quantities of lead, cadmium, cobalt, and gold, which sometime in the future can also be extracted.

Commercial interest began to assert itself in the mid-1960s. Since 1971, a comprehensive multidisciplinary exploration program has been conducted by the German mining concern Preussag AG, with the research ships *Valdivia* and *Sonne,* both of which we have met in earlier chapters. In 1975, after some legal uncertainties and conflicting claims, the two states bordering the Red Sea at the latitude of the mineral deposits, Saudi Arabia and the Sudan, formed the Saudi-Sudanese Joint Red Sea Commission as a common enterprise to mine the metals. They contracted with Preussag for the technical work of exploring, mining, and processing the metals. In this unique international joint venture, the Sudan and Saudi Arabia provide the resource, Saudi Arabia provides the capital, and Germany provides the technology, organization, and know-how. This arrangement is in many ways exemplary since all the partners stand to gain. Saudi Arabia benefits from industrial diversification and a decrease in its dependence on oil exports; the Sudan from the acquisition of technology and know-how; the Federal Republic of Germany reaps financial rewards from the utilization of their technology developed by one of its enterprises.

The work already accomplished is impressive indeed. How complex and multifaceted it is can best be described by following the work of *Valdivia* firsthand. In the spring of 1981 *Valdivia* completed the last of a series of three exploratory voyages, called MESEDA (*Me*talliferous *Sed*iments *A*tlantic II Deep), thereby concluding the first phase of exploration, research, and development. I was fortunate enough to be on the *Valdivia* as a guest of the commission during the final leg of the last voyage, sailing from Jeddah to Port Said and working for two weeks over the Atlantic II Deep, the Kebrit Deep area, and the northern Red Sea.

The *Valdivia* is an old stern-trawler which in 1971 was converted into a proud research ship. About 75 meters long, she displaces 2,115 tons, has a draft of 5.25 meters, and can maintain a maximum speed of 12 knots. Her comfortable air-conditioned cabins house a crew of twenty-four plus seventeen to nineteen scientists. Her wood-paneled mess room still radiates the cozy atmosphere of the old trawler days, but her eight scientific on-board laboratories—chemical, geological, geophysical, computer, photographic, compressor room, navigational, drawing—and two workshops, one mechanical, the other electronic, are equipped with the latest and most sophisticated technology.

There is a large working deck, sunny and breezy by day, floodlit by night, where the heavy gear is stored: cranes and winches; the multisampler, which brings up water from the depths; the piston corer, which penetrates the muds to a depth of 15 meters under 2 kilometers of water; the photo-sled that is towed over the seafloor at a speed of 2 knots, taking a color picture every five seconds; the plankton net; and the trawl for the macrofauna.

Work on this deck and in the labs goes on around the clock. The continuous activity and the ocean environment dissolves the traditional notion of time. On board *Valdivia*, one becomes detached from time, a detachment in part caused by the lack of any spatial reference points on the closed circle of the horizon, blue under the vault of the scorching skies.

"Deep is the well of the past." As we bring up water from the depth of the seafloor, what is left of my sense of time vanishes altogether. The infinite blue of the Red Sea today could be that of the Atlantic Ocean about 190 million years ago, when it began to open in the Gulf of Mexico and what are now North America and Africa began to part. For that is the stage at which the Red Sea is today: a nascent ocean, growing as the Arabian and the African tectonic plates drift apart. A rift, or graben, has begun to open in the middle of the sea, spewing molten lava that separates new oceanic crust, pushing the continents apart about 1 or 2 centimeters every year.

Cold sea water penetrates deep into the mantle of the earth, where it heats up and absorbs the metals and minerals of the interior. Like a geyser on dry land, the water returns to the seafloor. Meeting the cold bottom waters, it cools, and some of the minerals and metals precipitate and form sediments. The piston corer shows us the results of this process: layer upon layer of metal-bearing deposits, each with its own color and composition. There are dark brown manganese oozes; small thin beds of limonite oozes, ochre or light orange in color; limonite oozes enriched with foraminifera—winged snails; and abundant small chips of basaltic glass.

The strong net we fit to the sturdy frame of the closing trawl is certainly of our time and age. But with the floor of the Red Sea today resembling that of the Atlantic 190 million years ago, it is as if it will sink through millennia after being heaved over the stern by the powered winch. We follow its descent into the distant past on the "echo-profiler." Sonar beams are directed from the ship to the seafloor and their reflection is recorded and plotted as echo profiles, clearly showing the ups and downs of the hilly seafloor. The trawl is equipped with a "pinger," which also signals its exact location, plotted on a continuous line. When the pinger line and the seafloor echo-profile line meet, the trawl has reached the bottom, and it is slowly dragged over the rugged terrain. Sometimes it capsizes. Sometimes its net is torn. Once it came up with a full ton of mud and sands which had to be washed out all night long before what life there was on the seafloor could be recovered. It was as though we were the new gold washers of the old Wild West. And just as gold was found to be scarce, so life down there on the seabed was very thinly spread. The ton of mud we dredged from the floor yielded just one small tray of living matter.

What the trawl brings up is life as it was 190 million years ago, unchanged: a deep-sea spider and two solitary black corals, a couple of deep-sea eels, a luminous sardine and an odd little fish called Bembrops, with small eyes and a big mouth; a small urchin, sponges, and some krill-like shrimps, with small but functional eyes. They must be feeding on luminous prey, down there in the eternal night.

Amazingly, the shrimps are still alive, having survived the rough ascent through 2 kilometers of water. The difference in pressure did not kill them, as it does fish equipped with swim bladders. Fish often die due to the difference, not of pressure, but of water temperature. But one of the peculiarities of the Red Sea is that the temperature along the whole water column is just about the same (except for the brine pools), and thus the shrimps survived the voyage from the depths of the past.

So the days go by. Or are they weeks, or months? The water is blue and very transparent. The ship plows through schools of purple jellyfish. Silvery glistening mackerel keep them company. Once in a while a flying fish lands on our deck. At other times a bird.

The birds are tired. They must have flown over hundreds of kilometers of desert and sea before alighting on our deck. They must have lost their flock of migratory com-panions. They are forlorn and exhausted, so much so that they have no energy left to be afraid. Or have we gone back to a time when the beasts of the fields and the sky had yet to learn to fear man?

This is *Valdivia*'s fifth cruise to explore the mineral wealth of the Red Sea floor and to assess the possibilities of mining and processing it economically and without detriment to the delicate ecology of this sea. *Valdivia* began her exploratory work in 1971. The first part of her mission was to locate and map the deposits, to throw some light on their genesis, and to develop new technology and methodology. The Atlantis II Deep, the southern Red Sea, the Gulf of Aden, and the Gulf of Tadjoura were covered during the first expedition (VA 01). When it became clear that the Atlantis II Deep offered the best chances for successful exploitation, *Valdivia*'s second expedition to the Red Sea (VA 03, 1972) concentrated on that area and greatly expanded and deepened work in coring, hydrography, temperature measurements, and systematic mapping of the area.

To give an idea of the intensity of this work, suffice it to mention that during these two voyages 33,000 bathymetric profiles were taken and 1,500 meters of sediment corings were drawn. The results of this research were published in about eighty scientific papers.

The work was continued with the expeditions MESEDA I, II, and III, under contract to the Saudi-Sudanese Red Sea Commission. Concurrent with MESEDA II, a pilot mining test was carried out by the US drilling ship *SEDCO 445*—a ship, as we saw earlier, of nodule fame—which was prepared for this new mission in March 1979 in a shipyard in Marseilles. Seventeen carloads of specially designed equipment and instruments were sent by train from Germany.

There are basic similarities between the physical problems and technical solutions for raising manganese nodules and those for raising metalliferous muds from the seabed. Basically the same types of gear can be used. But there are differences. The depth of the nodule deposits is considerably greater than the depth of the metalliferous muds. The nodules have to be raised from 4,000 to 5,000 meters, the muds from a mere 2,000 meters. This, of course, makes things easier. On the other hand, the nodules are surficial, only one layer deep on the surface of the ocean floor, whereas the muds are layered, 10 to 15 meters deep. This makes both exploration and exploitation more difficult.

The mud-mining system, as shown in Figure 11, is in fact very similar to the one developed for nodule mining. The main difference is in the mining head. The mud-mining device has an oil-filled suction head con-

12. Schematic view of the autoanalyzer system

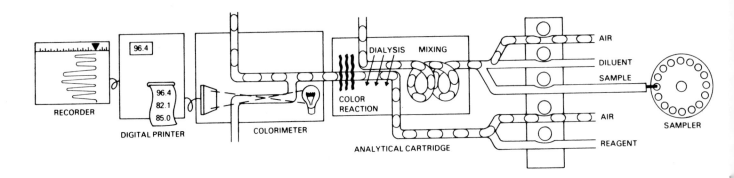

RECORDER
DIGITAL PRINTER
96.4
96.4
82.1
85.0
COLORIMETER
COLOR REACTION
ANALYTICAL CARTRIDGE
DIALYSIS   MIXING
AIR
DILUENT
SAMPLE
AIR
REAGENT
SAMPLER

taining an underwater electric motor which generates a vertical oscillation movement, to force penetration into the sediment layers by destroying the physical structure and liquefying the mud with a high-pressure jet of water. It takes about sixty seconds, after the motor has been turned on, before actual mining can start. The first hot brine, which covers the mud, arrives on deck after about 15 to 20 minutes, having traveled at a speed of 1.8 to 2.5 meters per second. Meter by meter the suction head burrows into the mud and turns up thickly liquefied mud—about 100 grams solids per liter of slurry. Although a number of technical problems arose, such as oil leaks, corrosion, and electrical problems, about 15,000 tons of mud and brine mixture were brought up successfully, demonstrating that a daily average of 200,000 tons could be achieved.

The next step was to reduce this mass and concentrate the metals, since it would be utterly uneconomical to ship such quantities in tankers to a distant processing plant. The problem was successfully solved through a process called flotation. The brine mixture is laid out on a bank of flotation "cells," and certain chemicals are added which adhere to the surface of the metal particles, making them water-repellant. The mixture is then agitated with paddle wheels, while air is bubbled in from below. The air bubbles carry the hydrophobic metal parts to the surface where they form a dark-colored foam which can be skimmed off by blades. This operation can be carried out continuously, processing 1.5 tons per hour per cell. Two thousand tons of mud brine were thus reduced to 4 tons of salt-free dry concentrate, containing 25 to 40 percent zinc in addition to 6 percent copper and 800 grams of silver per ton.

While one problem was solved, however, another arose. What was to be done with the tremendous amount of tailings? About 90 to 95 percent of the mass originally raised from the seafloor would have to be returned. When mining takes place on a commercial scale, about 190,000 tons of fine-grained mud, saturated with caustic chemicals, will be discharged every single day! Can the fragile ecosystem of the Red Sea absorb such massive alterations?

This was one of the questions addressed by the MESEDA III expedition. Finding the answer involved an extensive program of environmental research, including plankton investigation, water analysis, benthos research, diffusion tests, current measurements, and the sampling of the tracers released during MESEDA II. All these activities formed part of one beautifully integrated program in different disciplines; different scientific approaches all converged in a single collaborative investigation. The other major focus of investigation during MESEDA III was to increase understanding of the deposits, especially metal grades and quantities. This involved coring for improved deposit evaluation. In previous voyages, coring had been

accomplished most successfully in the upper layers, between 2 and 3 meters deep. But at greater depths, the sampling was still totally inadequate. Thus, while at 2 to 3 meters, 4.1 data points were available per square kilometer, the data points available for 14 to 15 meters' depth were only 0.1 per square kilometer. The average over the entire depth range was 2.033 data per square kilometer. Experience with land mining shows that a data base of 10 data points per square kilometer over the entire depth range is needed for reasonably accurate deposit evaluation.

To provide an optimum design for sampling during MESEDA III, geostatistical methods were applied. On the basis of work already undertaken, a grid of 308 elements of 500 × 500 meters was constructed within the Atlantis II Deep area. Within these grid elements, resources were calculated, or rather estimated, for each meter section below the seafloor. This is time-consuming, complex, and tedious work, both quantitatively and qualitatively. There should be at least one sample point within each grid element, and substantial gaps in knowledge about the chemistry and thickness of the deeper layers have yet to be closed.

We were moored above the Thetis Deep, where a sample coring was scheduled. The huge, heavy piston, in its casing, was hoisted over the railing, erected vertically, and then lowered by crane. We followed its descent on the echo-profiler. During its long descent, however, the ship was set adrift by currents. Hills appeared on the echo profile. If the piston was not to be smashed against the hills, it had to be withdrawn immediately. Having rescued the piston, the next problem was to find our way back to the deep, and this turned out to be a matter of several hours. We were drifting, and the sophisticated navigation system upon which we relied was letting us down.

This navigation system, known as INDAS (*I*ntegrated *N*avigation and *D*ata-processing *S*ystem), has a number of components, such as radio and dead-reckoning based on the determination of the ship's speed by Doppler sonar and of heading by gyro-compass. The heart of the system, however, is satellite communication, but the exact location of a ship at sea can be fixed only when the satellite is within visual range of the ship. There are "satellite gaps" between the appearance of one of the six US Navy orbited satellites and the next.

There happened to be such a gap while we were drifting at an unknown distance from the Thetis Deep. After about two hours, our "star" rose: a satellite that crossed the night sky in twenty minutes. During that time, magnetic tape on board produced the exact location of the ship, the exact distance (7 nautical miles) from the point over the Thetis Deep we were seeking to reach, and the exact compass direction we would have to steer.

During the next hour we watched the hilly landscape below and, at last, the steep descent into the 1,920-meter abyss of the Thetis Deep. We had arrived. A buoy was set out so we should not lose the place again. The buoy, a "miniranger," is equipped with light, radio, and sonar, and we can receive its signals within a 10- to 15-kilometer range.

Then the mighty piston corer was again hoisted overboard and lowered into the deep. We followed its descent on the screen: then, its return. Under the floodlights, it was brought back to rest in its casing alongside the railing of the working deck. The heavy screws were loosened, and its top lifted by crane.

But it was empty. All it contained was a few pieces of basaltic rock. It had hit the ground too close to the basaltic wall of the deep.

As the next day dawned, the cumbersome job had to be repeated. This time the corer brought up 2 meters of layered material. But only 2 meters, not the required 15.

This episode serves to illustrate the laboriousness of the work involved in obtaining the required data basis of 10 data points per square kilometer, down to a depth of 15 meters!

Bottom samples, on a smaller scale, can also be obtained by other means. There are the box grabbers, holding from 20 up to 1,000 liters of mud. The box grabber penetrates only the upper layers of sediments, but it brings the surface up undisturbed: a piece of the surface as it is *in situ*, with its micro- and macrofauna. When the box is set down safely by the crane on the working deck and opened, there is a race among the scientists on board to get there first. Each carries his own special collection of buckets, trays, tubes, and syringes. Within a minute the mass of mud comes to resemble a porcupine, spiked with test tubes and syringes.

The launching and recovery of the box grabber are the source of some excitement. Although small and comparatively light, its journey can be hazardous. Once, the chain to which it was attached almost broke. Had it broken, the instrument might have been lost. Had it crashed on deck, someone might have been seriously hurt.

Much greater yet is the excitement accompanying the launching and recovery of the really heavy gear, such as the piston corer, the stern-trawl, and the photo-sled. Here, too, the unexpected can occur. Once the large crane that was to recover the sled broke down, and those of us on the working deck were treated to an unplanned oil shampoo. On another occasion, the stern-trawl mistakenly collected a very heavy load of mud. It was an enormous job to right and steady the net and to pull it up the stern ramp. In this age of sophisticated, computerized, and automated research technology, it is surprising to see just how much heavy manual and skilled labor is required to enable it to function properly. And just how many risks and hazards there are to equipment and even to persons.

The easiest and least time-consuming method for obtaining samples from the sea-floor is the free-fall grabber, also called the "boomerang" or, more affectionately, the "boomy." It is a relatively light and handy instrument. To prepare it for launching, two weights are attached at the bottom, one on each side of the open jaws. It is then thrown

Atlantis II.

Red Sea cores.

Red Sea cores.

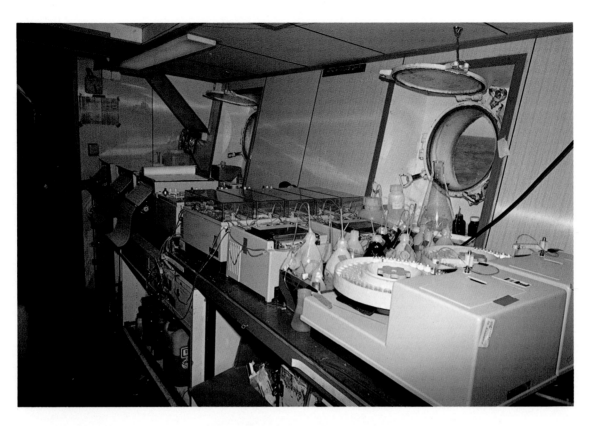

Autoanalyzer on board the *Valdivia*.

The television control center of *Valdivia*.

Below:
Preparing a bottom trawl.

Opposite above:
Research vessel *Valdivia* in the central Pacific.

Opposite below:
A bottom trawl.

Deep sea navigation buoy.

Right:
Servicing a solar-cell-powered navigation buoy.

Three generations of oil rig in the Red Sea.

overboard. When it hits the bottom, the jaws automatically close and the weights become detached. Glass spheres, attached above the grabber, provide the buoyancy required to enable it to return to the surface. It is equipped with a battery-powered signal light as well as with radio, which indicates where it can be picked up.

The "boomy" had been gone for a couple of hours, while everyone on board went about his business. We stood on the bridge in the beautiful, calm, moonlit night, scanning the horizon for its light. "There." The captain pointed to a luminous object in the far distance. *Valdivia* steamed in the direction of the faint light, and half an hour later, the "boomy" was lassoed and heaved over the rail by the crane. It contained 20 liters of surface muds. We were lucky: quite often it returns empty-jawed. Sometimes the weights release too early and the jaws close without grabbing anything at all. At other times the ground is too hard for a grab. On yet other occasions, the grabber loses most of its prey while closing. Or part of the sample may be washed out during the ascent. In spite of the time and labor it saves, some of our scientists on board do not think very highly of the "boomy."

A large part of the sampling material— mud, water, flora and fauna—is packed away and will be processed and analyzed on land, either because the necessary equipment is not available on board or because the ship's motion makes certain types of precision work impossible. However, many types of analyses are conducted in the ship's laboratories. Half of the cores are stirred up and homogenized in the geology lab and analyzed meter by meter of depth for wet density, water content, the amount of salt-free solids, and for the percentage of the various minerals and metals—iron, manganese, zinc, copper, silver, silicon, calcium, etc. The samples are evenly distributed between Preussag, the Saudi-Sudanese Red Sea Commission, and the German government, which sponsors the biological/environmental aspects of the project. One portion will be put

into cold storage for documentation. Each sample is described in a "core log," with a color photograph and an exact description (color, substance, texture) for each layer of sediment.

It is heartening indeed that such a considerable part of the exploration program is devoted to the biological/environmental impacts of seabed mining. These studies are carried out by marine scientists from a number of institutions in Germany and England, as well as in the Sudan and Saudi Arabia, both of which now have excellent marine scientific institutions. These studies are government-sponsored, independent of industry, and the scientists involved are free to publish their findings.

There is a growing awareness of, and concern about, environmental problems among the states bordering the Red Sea. Pollution from domestic sewage in coastal areas, industrial wastes, the dredging of harbors and waterways, and oil contamination have been increasing ominously over the past decades. While negotiating a protocol on the protection of the Red Sea and its coastal areas, the coastal states obviously want to make sure that the raising of the metalliferous muds from the bottom of the sea will not constitute an additional source of large-scale pollution.

The studies undertaken on board are most comprehensive, and the technologies employed are amazing in their complexity and sophistication. Our mission on MESEDA III included, among others, the following environment-related tasks:

• to increase statistical reliability of information on the amount of zooplankton, bacteria, and nutrients;
• to obtain quantitative information on the microfauna (drifting and free-swimming) of the deeper ocean layers;
• to investigate the trophic relationship among this microfauna and their interaction with the food web of the surface fauna;
• to detect seasonal changes in the intensity

and extent of diurnal vertical migration of zooplankton living in the mid-water layer (with the lowest oxygen content) and the deep-water zone below it;

• to deepen information on interrelationships between the plankton living in the area of the Atlantis II Deep and that of the northern Red Sea;

• to provide preliminary information on the variability from year to year in the pelagic ecosystem of the Atlantis II Deep area by comparison with data gathered by standardized methods on previous expeditions.

To assess the impact of mining and of the disposal of tailings on the ecosystem of the Red Sea, one obviously has to have as much information as possible on the existing situation and on ecosystem behavior under natural conditions. One has to know, for instance, something about the interaction between vertical layers and the up-and-down movements which might cause mud clouds to move upward rather than allowing them to sink to the bottom, and one has to examine the possibilities of pollution spreading from the mining areas in the Atlantis II Deep to the northern part of the Red Sea.

It is also vitally important to study the natural variations in the system, for example, the large-scale killing of fish by the periodic bloom of a blue-green alga—an extremely primitive single-celled plant called *Trichodesmium,* whose color is actually red, and which is responsible for the name of the "Red Sea." Such natural variations have to be taken into account when studying the impact of man-made interference. Calculations are often based on the assumption that the natural system is stable, and that it is destabilized by human intervention. If one more realistically assumes that the natural system itself is variable, then it becomes far more difficult—sometimes impossible—to calculate the impact of human intervention. Under certain conditions such intervention may reinforce variability and change. Under other circumstances, it may have a destabilizing effect which, given the variability of the system,

may actually contribute toward its stabilization. It is conceivable, but not very likely, for example, that man might release a pollutant that specifically killed *Trichodesmium.* If it did, the alga would be destroyed and the fish, killed by the alga when it blooms, would be saved.

To achieve the sixfold purpose, problems were attacked with different, converging approaches.

The larger sea animals, or macrofauna, are photographed by the photo-sled, brought up by the trawl, and sieved from the top layer of the box grabber. The thousands of photographs taken during each expedition give a fairly clear picture of the distribution of life and the groupings of various specimens for analysis and indicates the quantity over a given area. At one point, to the joyful excitement of the zoologist aboard, the trawl brought up a shrimplike creature that refused to be classified: no one had ever seen one like it before. "On the northern transects, however, new information on hard-bottom fauna was gathered from dredged pieces of rocks and corals," the board report reads. "For the first time a small xanthid crab was collected from a rock crevice." It was conserved in a formalin solution, to be taken to Frankfurt for further study, including comparison with the fauna of the Indian Ocean and the Mediterranean, to determine endemism in the Red Sea and patterns of transit from the Indian Ocean to the Mediterranean.

The sieving of the undisturbed surface layers in the boxgrabber reveals the distribution of living beings below the seafloor. Life ceases to exist about 15 centimeters below the surface. At greater depth the muds are too old, although none of the sediments in this nascent ocean are older than 25,000 years. The tiny animals, or microfauna, are brought in with a plankton net from the upper layers of the water (pelagic microfauna).

For the microfauna on the seafloor (benthic fauna), a series of most ingenious tests has been devised. One such test consists of the isolation and counting of enzymes from various centimeters of mud. An enzyme is any of various proteinlike substances, formed in plant and animal cells, that act as organic catalysts initiating or accelerating specific chemical reactions. Enzymes are present in large numbers in all living beings, and some of them relate to their respiration. The study of the change in enzyme activity may thus provide an early warning system for pollution.

A method for isolating enzymes has been developed by the biologists at the University of Hamburg. Although the method involves the use of the most sophisticated machinery, it also demands hours and hours of painstaking manual precision work for the preparation of the material. Carefully measured slices of mud are homogenized by high-frequency sound waves which smash all living cells and reduce the mud—microfauna, bacteria, and all—into a brownish cream. This is then centrifuged for ten minutes, which allows the sediments to settle at the bottom. A transparent liquid containing the enzymes separates out on top, clear as water. This is skimmed off and put into other glasses. The residue is discarded. A large number of test tubes are prepared with various chemicals. The enzymes are poured into them and the tubes are heated in a special machine. The chemicals dye the enzymes red: the redder the fluid, the more enzymes there are. Their number is calculated by computer on the basis of color intensity. The number of enzymes varies according to distance. The top centimeter of mud has twice as many enzymes as the centimeter below it. The red is thus most intense for the top centimeter, fading to nothing by the time the fifteenth centimeter is reached.

In a parallel experiment conducted in this busy lab, a biologist measures the oxygen consumption of the biomass inhabiting each centimeter slice of mud. The mud is placed in water kept at the exact temperature of its place of origin and the oxygen consumption is measured by electrodes.

The results of both tests, enzyme activity and oxygen consumption, are plotted by computer. The resulting graphs closely coincided, one test thus corroborating the other in determining the amount of biomass.

A third scientist, meanwhile, put his samples into a freezer. At his Hamburg University lab he will use his fine precision scales to establish the protein weight for each centimeter of depth. His computer graph should match the other two.

At the same time, hydrological studies proceeded in other labs. These make use of the multisonde data processor and the autoanalyzer, two of the ship's most recent pieces of high-technology equipment (Figures 12 and 13). The data processor is used to determine the physical parameters of sea water, its light-attenuation, pressure, temperature, conductivity, salinity, and oxygen content. The autoanalyzer is used to measure its chemical properties, especially nutrient content, an indication of the water's biological productivity.

All data, as recorded and stored by the on-board computers, are forwarded to Preussag's data processing center, which already contains millions of individual data on the physical and chemical parameters of the Atlantis II Deep sediments.

Other hydrological studies are devoted to current measurements. The direction and intensity of the ocean currents will obviously influence the settling of the sediments dumped from the mining ship. Surface currents are measured by drifting buoys (drogues) of various sizes. Other technologies are employed to measure the currents down to a depth of 500 meters. Particularly useful are "profilers," which are lowered on a cable and take measurements every 30 seconds during the descent. Special modifications are needed for the operation of current meters at the high temperatures of the brines at the bottom of the sea. At very great depth, only conical cables can be used since cylindrical cables would snap by their own weight!

In spite of all the work done, the nature of Red Sea currents is as yet little understood. The profilers appear to have established, however, that current intensities diminish at greater depth, whereas they increase sharply near the seafloor (brine currents).

In 1979, during MESEDA II, *SEDCO 445* released 800 tons of sediments at a depth of 400 meters. Before dumping, the scientists of MESEDA II took 50 tons of these sediments and mixed them with 1,000 grams of powdered iridium, a rare metal belonging to the platinum family. Since iridium has never been found in the Red Sea, its use in powdered form was considered suitable as a tracer.

A year and a half after releasing the tracers, the sediments were analyzed for their iridium content. The testing proceeded in concentric circles within 1,000 square kilometers around the dumping site. Assuming that the iridium was perfectly homogenized within the sediment, and assuming homogeneous sedimentation over a total sea-bottom area of 1,000 square kilometers, one can calculate that there should be 10^{-6} grams of iridium per square meter of sea bottom. At least a hundred samplings would be necessary to establish this fact. Only twelve were in fact taken. Given the number of tests, the uncertainty of the basic assumptions, and the imperfection of sampling methods, the evidence must be considered inconclusive.

The scientists of MESEDA III turned sad and silent when they recalled the dumping experiment. A cloud, perhaps carried up by the diurnal vertically migratory plankton, covered kilometers of the ocean's surface and lingered for weeks, perhaps months. The scientists surmised that the cloud must have done considerable damage to sea life over a vast area. If dumping is to take place, they suggested, it probably would have to be done at a greater depth: at least 800 meters below the surface, below the planktonic zone, which ends at 700 meters. Whether this is feasible is, more than anything else, a question of cost.

In the meantime, *Valdivia* was nearing Suez, and MESEDA III was coming to an end. Instruments and samples were packed away and we returned to the real world of people, places, and time. The blue vault of the sky was again full of all the reference points we needed.

What has been evoked in these pages is but a meager extract from the copious notes I took during the journey. My notes, moreover, fail to do justice to the enormous body of scientific and technical information put together during the expedition. I am not a scientist, and in spite of the patient explanations and demonstrations provided by the scientists on board and the openness with which they encouraged me to take an active part in their work, there was much that remained a mystery to me, just as it would be a mystery to most of the readers of this book. The box grabber had been down twenty-three times at eight locations; the photo-sled spent some ten hours on the seafloor, in five locations; the closing trawl had explored five locations (the same as the photo-sled); the piston corer, three locations; and there had been six water stations plus a whole aquarium-full of surface water pumped into about a hundred canisters from a rubber raft. And this all happened during the final (ninth) leg of a voyage that lasted five months. One has to multiply these numbers by nine in order to get a real idea of the amount of work undertaken in one expedition, MESEDA III.

No doubt the work had been successful, and the mining project will move on to the next stage. A second mining test is needed to bring production up to a commercial scale. Exploration, refinement of the data base, economic evaluation, environmental research, and the building of a land-based processing plant must all go ahead. From the perspective of the mining technology as such , full-scale commercial production could begin before the end of the decade. There are, however, two caveats:

The first is the world economic situation. Should it continue to deteriorate and metal markets remain depressed, there will be little economic incentive to create a new mining industry while the old ones are ailing. This applies just as much to the Red Sea muds as it does to the nodules of the Pacific ocean floor.

The second is the environmental impact. Current measurements and research on benthos, plankton, fish, and reefs will continue, hand in hand with a variety of water analyses and tests on muds and tailings. The construction of an integrated environmental computer model designed to study impacts is planned. But still one wonders. Is it a good idea to bring up 200,000 tons of mud from a depth of 2 kilometers, just to dump 185,000 back again, with all the contingent problems? It does not seem economical. It does not seem to be the most practical way of going about things.

The first motor-car builders put the mo-

13. Shipboard processing of multisonde data

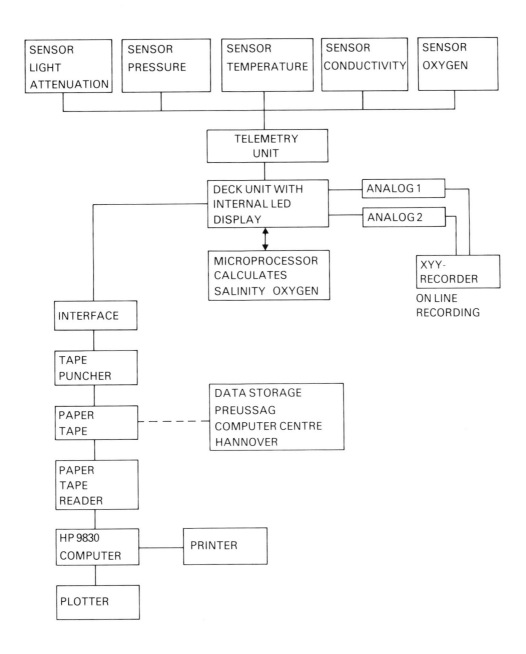

tor in front of the car, simply because the horse had been in front of the buggy. Horsepower, whether natural or man-made, was to be applied in front of the car, no matter the problems in transmitting it to the rear wheels. It took generations of car builders to realize that it could be more practical to put the motor in the rear; and then only a few really did it.

That processing has to be done on the surface of the earth is perhaps an ingrained prejudice of the kind that put motors in front of cars. Perhaps the system is quite impractical, however, when applied to ocean mining.

At a time when processing can take place in automated factories in satellites in outer space, would it not be possible to do it 2,000 meters down in inner space? Could not the Navy's Sealab technologies be adapted to this practical purpose? Could not the burgeoning robot industry be employed?

Certainly the high pressure might create problems for processes like flotation. Yet I have an idea that it could be easier to solve these problems—or even to put them to advantageous use, just as weightlessness is used in outer-space processing—than to attempt to solve the ones created by lifting 200,000 tons of mud every day from the ocean floor and depositing most of it back where it came from.

To collect, process, and concentrate *in situ,* through automated equipment, supervised, perhaps, by one diver, and to raise 10,000 tons of concentrate a day rather than 200,000 tons of muds and brine would mean incredible savings in energy, the elimination of technological hazards, and the solution of environmental problems. The resulting financial savings could well justify the additional costs of research and development.

But first we have to get used to the fact that an automobile is not a horse and buggy, and that the motor may be better in the rear even though the horse is in front!

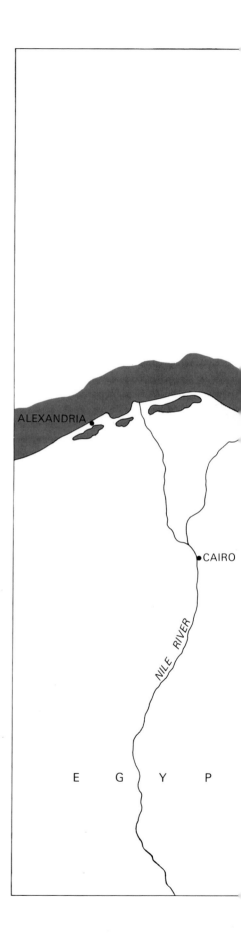

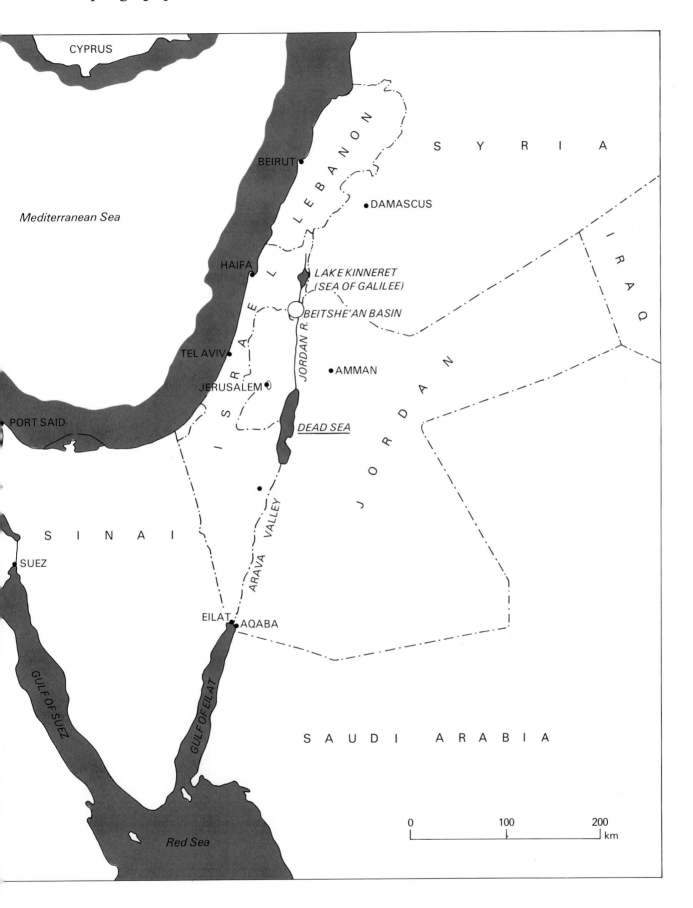

Low tide, Bay of Fundy.

⧘ Chapter 5 ⧘
THE FIRE AND THE FORGE

On the map before me, the top part of the Red Sea looks like a fleshy lobster claw, with the Gulf of Suez and the Gulf of Aqaba like the two shears of the scissors. The Suez shear has an extension: a lumpy thread running north to Port Said, where it reaches the Mediterranean. It is, of course, the Suez Canal. It bulges at the sealike Bitter Lakes, where rows of cargo ships, tankers, and some research ships are moored, waiting their turn to pass in convoy through the one-way traffic lanes.

It is not only ships that follow the gentle currents of the man-made link between the Indo-Pacific and Mediterranean-Atlantic ocean systems. Fish do the same, as do other fauna and flora, with consequences as yet unfathomed. The changes in the fauna and flora of the Mediterranean resulting from the opening of the Suez Canal were, however, slow to come about. A twofold natural barrier closed the road of man to the transmigration of nature.

The Red Sea is saltier than most oceans—only the Dead Sea is known to be saltier—and within the Red Sea the Bitter Lakes are the most saline. Layers of salt line the bottom of the lakes; 970 million tons of salt sediments saturate their waters. The canal has a salinity of 76 to 80 per mil, compared to the 43 percent of the Red Sea. Few fish could penetrate this barrier. Those that succeeded could try to regain their internal balance during the next 150 kilometers or so of their wandering down to Port Said. But

there a second trial lay in wait for them: the Nile delta's right arm, which poured masses of fresh water into the sea and into the path of the migrating fish. The water in which they found themselves on entering the Mediterranean was so desalinated—down to about 26 per mil—that few could withstand it. If the salinity of the environment does not closely correspond with the salinity of the body fluids, the fish, our epic traveler, dies the death of osmotic implosion or explosion.

Just as Tamino and Tamina had to pass trial by fire and trial by water before reaching the end of their road in *The Magic Flute*, so the fish transmigrating from the Indo-Pacific to the Mediterranean had to pass the tests of hypersalinity and hyposalinity. The Taminos and Taminas among the fish were few and far between. During the first sixty years of the canal's existence, only a few species were successful in overcoming the barriers to their transmigration.

But meanwhile, mankind continued in its beaverlike way to transform the environment. The canal was repeatedly deepened, which increased the strength of the current. The Bitter Lakes were flushed and the salt leached from the bottom. Salinity decreased to about 43 to 46 per mil, coming very close to that of the Red Sea. At the other end, the construction of the Aswan Dam reduced the flow of fresh water entering the Mediterranean. Salinity in the Port Said area rose to 39 to 40 per mil. The roadblocks were thus cleared and the fish traffic became denser. In the two decades between 1960 and 1980 nine times more species transmigrated than in the preceding six decades.

This heralds a true revolution in the flora and fauna of the Mediterranean. Whether for good or for evil will largely depend upon our understanding and the steps we take on the basis of this understanding. Some of the new species are food fish and may increase the productivity of the relatively depopulated waters of the Mediterranean Sea. Others—fish as well as algal newcomers—might be noxious and compete with the indigenous fauna and flora. The mineral composition and the hydrology of the Mediterranean might in the long run be affected. Here is a field for the application of "aquaculture" in the broadest sense: for systemic intervention, on a regional scale, that might yield large dividends in food and fiber, in minerals and energy.

The other shear of the scissors, ending at Eilat and Aqaba, finds its prolongation in the Arava Valley, widening into the Dead Sea. Here the Jordan River ends its course from the Lebanese mountains across the Beitsche'An Basin and the Sea of Galilee.

If the Red Sea represents the infancy of an ocean system, the Dead Sea is an ocean in the prenatal stage. Its length is a mere 96 kilometers, compared to the Red Sea's 2,000. Its width never exceeds 6 kilometers and its maximum depth is 400 meters (Figure 14).

The Dead Sea is remarkable for two reasons. First, its surface, lying almost 400 meters below sea level, constitutes the lowest point on the earth's surface. Second, its waters are "denser," being richer in salts and other minerals and metals, than any other large body of water. Like the sap of a wheat germ or bean sprout, containing the potential of a grown plant, the embryonic Dead Sea waters seem to hold the mineral contents of a full-grown ocean.

The ancients certainly noticed its peculiarities. The Greek physician Galen observed that its waters appeared whiter and heavier than most seas, this whiteness periodically resulting from the precipitation of calcium carbonate (plaster). Modern oceanography has estimated that the amount of calcium carbonate can within a few days, usually in August, increase to some 5 million tons. The total amount of dissolved salts in the Dead Sea is almost 44 billion tons. Far more than that, however, is encrusted in layers under the sea floor, certainly accessible to modern mining technology.

The "technology" to extract salts from sea water is ancient. It goes back thousands of years and involves the oldest known use of solar energy. The sea water trapped at high tide in small basins, pools, holes, and cavities was simply allowed to evaporate, leaving behind salt crystals, either partly broken down into a white grainy mass or in sheet form, overlying a residue of sea water. All man had to do was to collect the results of this natural process.

The Chinese extracted sea salts as far back as 2200 B.C. The kings of India had a "superintendent of ocean mines" as early as the fourth century B.C. It was his responsibility to "attend to the collection of conch shells, diamonds, precious stones, pearls, corals, and salt and also regulate the commerce in the above commodities." This is prescribed in Kautiliya's *Arthasastra,* a treatise on government from the period 321–296, which has only recently been rediscovered. "Soon after crystallization of salt is over," the book continues, "the superintendant of salt shall in time collect both the money rent and the quantity of shares of salt due to the government; and by the sale of salt (thus collected as shares) he shall realize not only its value but also the premium of five percent, both in cash." There are numerous additional details regarding financial arrangements and fines. It is stipulated, for instance, that "adulteration of salt shall be punished with the highest amercement; likewise, persons other than hermits manufacturing salt without licence." Special regard not only for religion but also for learning, as well as for labor, is shown in the provision that "men learned in the Vedas, persons engaged in penance, as well as labourers may take with them salt for food; salt and alkalis for purposes other than this shall be subject to the payment of toll."

The Anglo-Saxons of the Iron Age were familiar with the craft of extracting salt from the sea, common to all people inhabiting the shores of warmer seas. In essence, the "technology" has not changed through the millennia, although it has become more sophisticated with the passage of time. Today, a system of ponds is used rather than a set of shallow pools. Sea water is first allowed to enter a series of "concentrating ponds," where muds and ferrous and calcinate compounds are sorted and a first concentration of the salts takes place. This concentrate is then passed through a second set of ponds where slaked lime is added and the calcium is precipitated out in the form of calcium sulfate or gypsum plaster. The remaining concentrate is led into a third set of ponds, the "harvesting ponds," where the remaining water is evaporated and the salt is extracted. The remaining brine, or "bittern," is pumped out and can be further "mined" for magnesium and potassium, which becomes a by-product of sea-salt mining.

One of the largest sea-salt mines in the world is at Guerrero Negro in Baja California (Mexico). Covering over 49,000 acres, this solar evaporation system contains 200 kilometers of dikes, 40 kilometers of canals, and 45 kilometers of main haul roads. The endless expanse of salt—salt as far as the eye can see, salt heaped into mountains, salt everywhere—looks like vast fields of snow. The salt crystals crunch underfoot just like ice crystals. The Mexicans export 6 million tons of sea salt annually to Japan.

Potassium is crucially important to the fertilizer industry. Where the potassium content of sea water is as abnormally high as it is in the Dead Sea, it is logical that mining it should have become an end in itself. The process of extracting potassium from the sea, perfected by an enterprising Russian, M. Novomeysky, in the 1920s and '30s, is basically similar to that of simple salt extraction. In his first large-scale plant, Palestine Potash

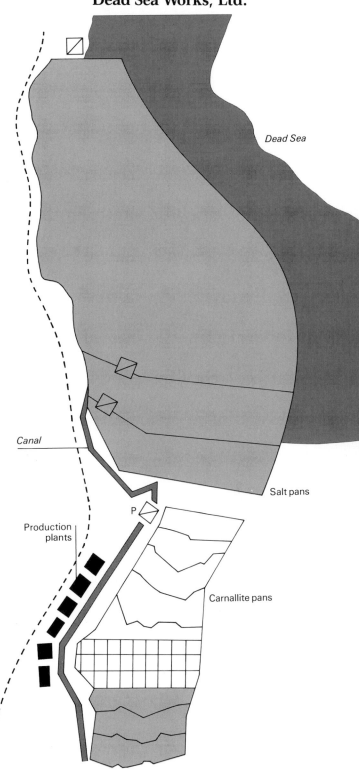

15. Scheme of solar pans at the Dead Sea Works, Ltd.

Dead Sea

Canal

Salt pans

Production plants

P

Carnallite pans

Overleaf:
Salt pans, Malta.

Ltd., at the northern tip of the Dead Sea, Novomeysky first passed the sea water through a set of large shallow evaporation pans, then through successively smaller ones, where the minerals were allowed to crystallize on the basis of their different solubilities.

Novomeysky's first solar evaporation potash extraction plant, located at Kallia on the East Bank of the Jordan River, commenced operations in 1930. By 1932 it was producing over 8,000 tons of potash and over 200 tons of bromine annually at highly competitive prices. Production increased tenfold during the next ten years and a second plant was constructed near Sedom, at the southern tip of the Dead Sea. By 1940, the UK's potash demand was filled almost totally by these two plants.

Both were damaged during the 1947/48 Palestinian war of independence. The new state of Israel, fully aware of the potential of export earnings from potash extraction, lost no time in rebuilding and modernizing the Sedom plant, which was given the name of "Dead Sea Works." Full-scale production started in 1955. A decade later, the Dead Sea Works was producing four times the amount of potash produced by the two plants together before the war. Its total capacity was 2 million tons (Figures 15 and 16). Bromine production also went up from 200 to 7,000 tons annually. In the 1970s, however, there was a worldwide overproduction of potash, the market began to decline, and production had to be cut back to adjust to falling export demand. Most of the high-potash-consuming industrialized countries are now self-sufficient. A number of countries have in fact begun to experiment with large-scale production techniques to extract potassium salts from the waters of other seas and oceans.

Salt and potassium, bromine, calcium and magnesium salts, gypsum and phosphates can be extracted from sea water by relatively simple methods using solar energy. But there is far more in Neptune's liquid mine. Sea water contains practically all the metals and minerals that can be found on

land. It is enough to remember that one cubic mile of sea water contains, among other things, 47 tons each of iron, aluminum, molybdenum, and zinc, 14 tons each of copper, tin, uranium, and arsenic, 9 tons of titanium, 2 tons each of antinomy, cobalt, caesium, and cerium—and there are 328,750,000 cubic miles of water in the oceans! More of the useful metals and minerals, their quantities and density, are listed in Table 8.

The production of metals and the production of energy are inseparably linked. Without fire there is no forge. Today our minds are still the captives of our terrestrial, mostly petroleum-based energy systems, and it is these that we are trying to apply to Neptune's forge. The mismatch is blatant. It does not have much future. Neptune's forge calls for Neptune's fire, and this may take a great variety of shapes.

The waters of the oceans hold enormous untapped energy resources. It is these that could be harnessed, with a minimum of environmental problems, to extract as much of the minerals and metals from the liquid mine as we may need.

The quantities of available ocean energy boggle the terrestrial mind. Those who believe in the future of nuclear energy can be comforted by the thought that "the total amount of fissionable uranium and thorium in seawater is sufficient to sustain the estimated 21st-century level of power production for some million of years," as John D. Isaacs and Walter R. Schmitt put it.

Still remaining within the nuclear sphere, one may assume that, by the beginning of the next century, nuclear energy will be produced by thermonuclear fusion, which is likely to avoid many of the hazards inherent in energy produced from nuclear fission, in particular the horrendous problems of waste disposal. Thermonuclear fusion will require lithium or deuterium. These, Isaacs and Schmitt continue, "are present in sufficient quantity to sustain that power level for the remainder of the life of the solar system."

Deuterium is also an essential ingredient

Table 8: Concentration of Elements in Sea Water

Element	Concentration (mg/l)	Amount of Element in Sea Water (t/m)	Total Amount in the Ocean (t)
Chlorine	19,000.0	89.5×10^6	29.3×10^{15}
Sodium	10,500.0	49.5×10^6	16.3×10^{15}
Magnesium	1,350.0	6.4×10^6	2.1×10^{15}
Sulfur	885.0	4.2×10^6	1.4×10^{15}
Calcium	400.0	1.9×10^6	0.6×10^{15}
Potassium	380.0	1.8×10^6	0.6×10^{15}
Bromine	65.0	306,000.0	0.1×10^{15}
Carbon	28.0	132,000.0	0.04×10^{15}
Strontium	8.0	38,000.0	$12,000.0 \times 10^9$
Boron	4.6	23,000.0	$7,100.0 \times 10^9$
Silicon	3.0	14,000.0	$4,700.0 \times 10^9$
Fluorine	1.3	6,100.0	$2,000.0 \times 10^9$
Argon	0.6	2,800.0	930.0×10^9
Nitrogen	0.5	2,400.0	780.0×10^9
Lithium	0.17	800.0	260.0×10^9
Rubidium	0.12	570.0	190.0×10^9
Phosphorus	0.07	330.0	110.0×10^9
Iodine	0.06	280.0	93.0×10^9
Barium	0.03	140.0	47.0×10^9
Indium	0.02	94.0	31.0×10^9
Zinc	0.01	47.0	16.0×10^9
Iron	0.01	47.0	16.0×10^9
Aluminum	0.01	47.0	16.0×10^9
Molybdenum	0.01	47.0	16.0×10^9
Selenium	0.004	19.0	6.0×10^9
Tin	0.003	14.0	5.0×10^9
Copper	0.003	14.0	5.0×10^9
Arsenic	0.003	14.0	5.0×10^9
Uranium	0.003	14.0	5.0×10^9
Nickel	0.002	9.0	3.0×10^9
Vanadium	0.002	9.0	3.0×10^9
Manganese	0.002	9.0	3.0×10^9
Titanium	0.001	5.0	1.5×10^9
Antinomy	0.0005	2.0	0.8×10^9
Cobalt	0.0005	2.0	0.8×10^9

SOURCE: Adapted from I. Kaplan, "Mater Omnium," p. 59.

of the nuclear fission process. Deuterium atoms are used to produce heavy water, which is used as a "moderator" in nuclear reactors, slowing down the neutrons released during the fission of uranium-235 atoms. When the neutrons are slowed down, they split other atoms of uranium 235 and thus sustain a chain reaction. Near-shore heavy-water factories separate the heavy water from normal sea water or fresh water (there being about 1 liter of heavy water in every 7,000 liters of natural water) through a chem-ical process employing hydrosulfide, a tremendously poisonous, instantly lethal gas.

To mine the oceans, however, ocean energy can be applied directly, without passing through terrestrial power plants. This can be done in a variety of ways. Tidal energy, wave energy, power generation through ocean currents, ocean thermal energy conversion, the utilization of salinity gradients, and marine-biological engineering have all been studied, experimented with, and some of them have been fully commercialized.

16. Chemical flowsheet of potassium chloride recovery

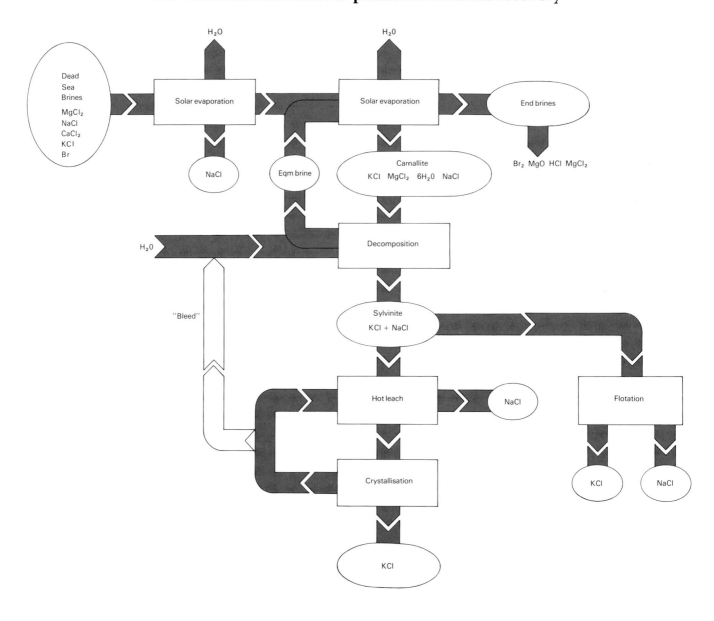

17. Sites with major potential for tidal power

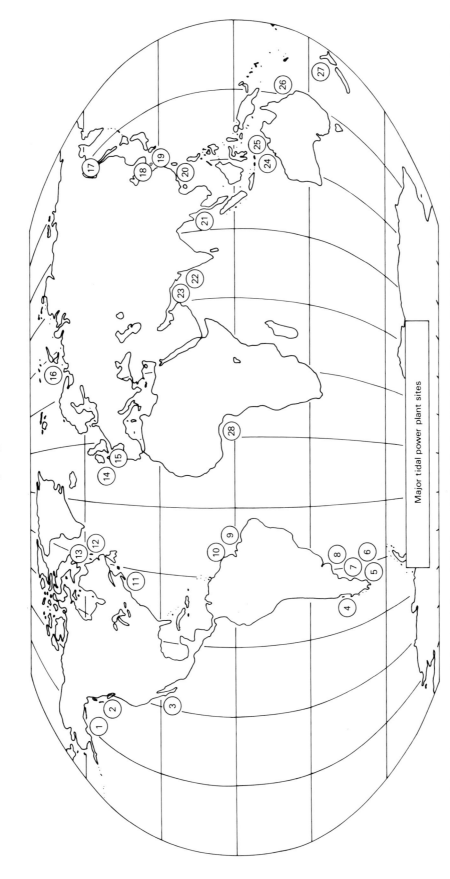

Major tidal power plant sites

1. Cook inlet;   2. British Columbia;   3. Baja California;   4. Chonos Archipelago;   5. Magellan Straits;   6. Gallegos/Sta Cruz;   7. Gulf of San Jorge;   8. Jan José Gulf;   9. Maranhao;   10. Araguaia;
11. Fundy/Quoddy;   12. Ungava Bay;   13. Frobisher Bay;   14. Severn/Solway;   15. Rance;   16. Mezen/Kislaya;   17. Okhotsk Sea;   18. Seoul River;   19. Shanghai;   20. Amoy;   21. Rangoon;
22. Cambay Bay;   23. Runn of Kutch;   24. Kimberleys;   25. Darwin;   26. Broad Sound;   27. Manukau;   28. Abidjan

121

Energy generation through tidal power has a long history. The Greeks used the tides of the Ionian Sea. The Anglo-Saxons built tide mills in Wales and in Dover Harbor in about A.D. 1100. They were located in small tidal basins or ponds in which tidewater was impounded. As it flowed back at ebb tide, it drove a wheel which activated a mill. The Dutch also used tide mills in the Zuiderzee at about the same time or a little later. They introduced them to New York in the seventeenth century. While theories on the origin and nature of tides go back to classical antiquity, the oldest known treatise on the utilization of tides is by an Italian, Mariano, published in 1438.

The power of the tides is enormous and has been variously estimated at between 300 and 450 terawatts per year (1 terawatt is equal to 1,000 gigawatts, or 10^6 megawatts, or 10^9 kilowatts, or 10^{12} watts). This power—or a modest part of it!—can be extracted in various ways. The incoming tide can be treated like one enormous wave, a wave of waves, and its vertical displacement can be utilized to raise a floating mass. As this mass falls back to its original position, it can do useful work. This has been called the "float method."

The tide can also be treated like a current or stream that is used to rotate a paddle wheel. This is the method applied in tide mills, which work like other waterwheels near waterfalls.

The third method is really a refinement of the second. Here, a part of the sea is dammed off and a basin created. This fills with the incoming tide and at low tide releases the water through turbines, either back into the sea or into another basin. Instead of applying tidal power on a small scale to drive a wheel, this power, on a larger scale, is used to drive a turbine/generator which generates electricity.

The most successful application of this method is the St.-Malo tidal energy plant at the mouth of the Rance River in northern France, built in 1969. The dam is about 1 kilometer long, and the basin encloses 22

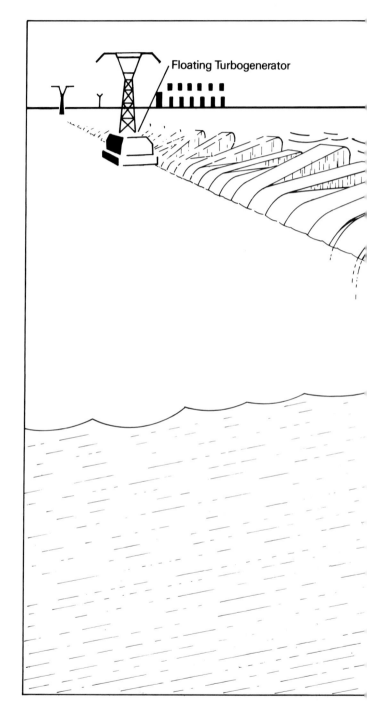

Floating Turbogenerator

18. Schematic view of "Salter's Duck" for harnessing wave power

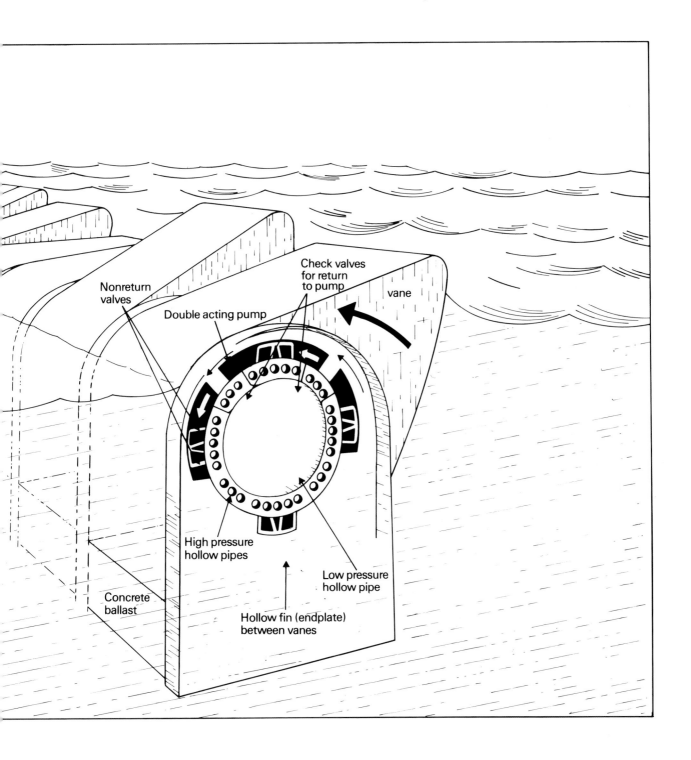

Nonreturn valves

Check valves for return to pump

vane

Double acting pump

High pressure hollow pipes

Low pressure hollow pipe

Concrete ballast

Hollow fin (endplate) between vanes

square kilometers, into which the tidal water rushes at a speed of up to 20,000 cubic meters per second! The turbines at the dam are equipped with reversing blades and are thus able to generate electricity both when the tide rushes in and when it goes out. About half a million kilowatts are generated with each tide, or about 500 gigawatts per year.

While the location of this plant is very favorable, there are a few places in the world with even greater potential. At St.-Malo, the average spring tide range is about 11.5 meters during new moons and full moons; the average during the lower part of the cycle—just after the first and the third quarter moon, the so-called neap tide—is about 5.4 meters. The biggest tides in the world are to be found in the Bay of Fundy in Canada, where the overall maximum range is about 16 meters, and the neap tides average about 7.3 meters. The annual output of one of the three possible sites for a plant is estimated at 12,653 gigawatts per hour, compared to 500 for St.-Malo. By 1990 it could account for one-half of the estimated world oil consumption for heating. Other advantages would be that the price of the energy would remain stable throughout the life span of the plant, whereas the price of oil is bound to keep increasing. It would lead to lower environmental pollution loads compared to electricity expansion programs without tidal power; and it would have spin-offs in research and development applicable not only to tidal power but to hydroelectric development in general. Canada is actively pursuing this project. It should be completed by 1990.

Other sites with great potential are Passamaquoddy Bay, close to the entry to the Bay of Fundy (although the tidal ranges are much lower); the Cook Inlet in Alaska; the Severn Estuary and Bristol Channel in England; the San José Gulf in Argentina; and numerous locations in the Soviet Union, India, Bangladesh, Australia, and China, where a number of small-scale projects have been realized in the past decades. Calculations made for the Kimberley coast of western Australia indicate that a plant located there could pro-

duce over 3×10^6 kilowatts, or about 50 times the present production of electricity in Australia. This, of course, is the reason why it has not yet been built: there is not yet a sufficient demand.

The Soviet Union has built an experimental plant in Kislaya Guba on the White Sea. The first installed turbine was made in France, but the USSR has been quite successful in acquiring this technology and is now a competitive exporter of turbines, not only for tidal plants but for other hydroelectric plants as well.

The electrical energy needs in the early twenty-first century are estimated at about 3×10^7 megawatts or 3×10^1 terawatts per hour per annum. According to the most conservative estimates, tidal power alone could provide 300 terawatts on a global basis. In theory, it would thus be possible to satisfy demand entirely with tidal energy. However, this might have very strange environmental consequences.

Due to natural "tidal friction," that is, a power loss of about 3 million megawatts annually, the earth's days are lengthening by about 1.5 milliseconds per century, and the radius of the moon's orbit is increasing ever so slightly. If this natural power loss is increased by the continuous "mining" of tidal energy, at a scale of 3×10 terawatts, even at 50 percent efficiency, the lengthening of the day would increase twentyfold, to 30 milliseconds per century, and the moon would gradually recede farther into the distance. But, as Isaacs and Schmitt rather wryly conclude, "The increased length of day of about five minutes per million years might be tolerable for the foreseeable future."

Tidal power, though potentially huge, is practically restricted to a few locations where, in some cases, it cannot be developed because of lack of demand. Wave power, on the other hand, is distributed all over the world's oceans and could contribute quite substantially to the global energy supply. It has been calculated that wave power can produce an average of 75 kilowatts per hour per meter of length of shoreline. On a global scale this would add up to something on the order of 2.5×10^{12} watts, or 2.5 terawatts. Research on wave power has been going on for several decades. It may take another twenty years of intensive research and development, however, before the exploitation of this potentially great energy source can be carried out on a fully commercial scale.

Wave power and tidal power technologies are related, and they overlap. A wave, or a train of waves, is in effect a small tide. It can be trapped, for instance by converging ramps, and funneled into a higher-lying basin. As the water recedes, its power can be utilized to drive a low-pressure turbine that generates electricity.

There are a number of different methods for exploiting wave power. Important centers of research are located in Japan, the UK, and the USA. Each one pursues a different approach.

The Japanese have perfected a wave-activated electricity generator called Ryoku-seisha TG-2. It utilizes the vertical displacement of the wave motion to compress an enclosed air supply which drives an air turbine directly connected to an electric generator. This type of gear is used to light navigational buoys, ocean survey instruments, etc. A large-scale power plant is being built in Japan on this principle.

In the United States, a variety of smaller-scale experiments have been carried out. Perhaps the most interesting is the one perfected by the Foundation for Ocean Research in San Diego. It appears to resolve some of the difficulties encountered in other methods, especially those caused by storms and exceedingly rough seas. The San Diego technology is very simple and weather-resistant. A buoy is connected to a long vertical pipe, which is flooded with water. The water in the pipe is forced upward by the motion of the buoy. This creates a hydraulic pressure, which in a 100-meter pipe may reach about 5 atmospheres. Before this pressure is reached, the water is released under pressure and drives a turbine and power is generated.

The potential for wave power along Brit-ain's Atlantic coast is such that 100 kilometers exploited at 30 percent efficiency would satisfy Britain's total electrical power requirements. In laboratory conditions, an efficiency of 90 percent has already been achieved with the "nodding duck," or "Salter's duck"—S. H. Salter of the University of Edinburgh being the inventor. Salter devised a sort of pear-shaped instrument, round at the landward side, pointed at the side facing the wave. The point is raised by the oncoming wave, which induces the round side to rotate downward. As the wave passes, the pointed side drops back to its original position, and the round part rotates back upward (Figure 18). This gives the instrument its "nodding" motion. A number of these devices are strung on a common axis, which needs to be at least 1 kilometer long to achieve the required balance. The whole array could be anchored or allowed to move landward, in which case it would have to be periodically towed back to its original position.

The UK has also invested considerable research and development funds in some other technologies. The "Russel rectifier" works like a mini tidal plant, with the waves trapped in a higher basin and released through turbines. A third project, Wave Power Ltd., is similar in concept to the San Diego one in that it works with hydraulic pressure. It makes use, however, of a series of rafts and converts their motion-energy into high pressure in a fluid.

The potential of wave power is thus very great. The present state of research and development seems to suggest, however, that at least for the immediate future it will be limited to small-scale applications, such as lights for buoys or the propulsion of ships. It could also provide power to small coastal communities, especially in developing countries.

Energy generation from ocean currents belongs to the same family of technology developed to capture the power of tides and waves. The difference is that this energy is even more diffused, and this poses particular problems.

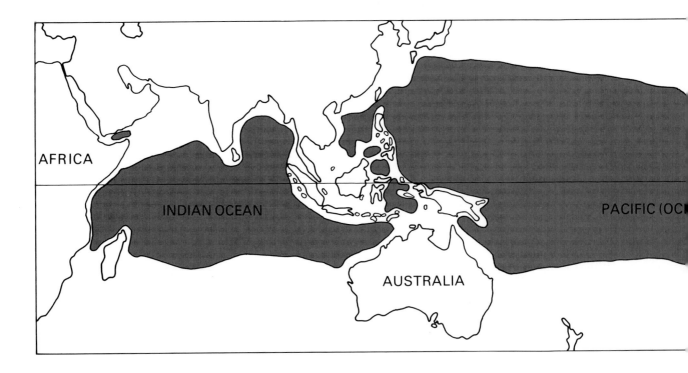

AFRICA

INDIAN OCEAN

PACIFIC (OC

AUSTRALIA

The world ocean is traversed by a system of immense rivers. Driven by winds, listing to the earth's rotation, these rivers, meandering without riverbeds or fixed boundaries, carry their water masses around the world: the Gulf Stream in the North Atlantic, the Japan Current in the North Pacific, the Brazil Current in the South Atlantic, the Agulhas in the Indian Ocean, and the East Australian Current in the South Pacific, to name some of the major ones.

The dimensions of these water masses are enormous. The Gulf Stream carries about 30 million cubic meters of water per second past Miami: more than five times the total flow of all fresh-water rivers of the planet put together! But the flow is slow, less than 1 meter per second on the average. While the total energy of the current passing Miami has been estimated to be about 25 gigawatts, perhaps only 4 percent of this could actually be extracted by low-pressure turbines, which would have to be placed between 30 and 130 meters below the surface across the 20 kilo-

meters of the Miami Terrace. "This array of machines," the proponents of the scheme suggest, "would deliver perhaps 1,000 million watts on a 24-hour basis," as much as two large nuclear plants.

Other mechanisms have been proposed by other researchers, but they are still on the drawing board or at best at the small laboratory-model scale. Should they be realized, they could be applied not only to slow-moving ocean currents but to large fresh-water rivers as well.

The potential of the remaining three approaches to the utilization of ocean energy is even more impressive. Let us begin with energy from biomass.

On land, the search for alternative energy resources has led to attempts to convert biomass, in the form of energy crops or the processing of waste organic materials, into liquid or gaseous fuel. City garbage conversion plants are beginning to make a contribution to the satisfaction of urban energy demands. Methane, methanol, ethanol, are

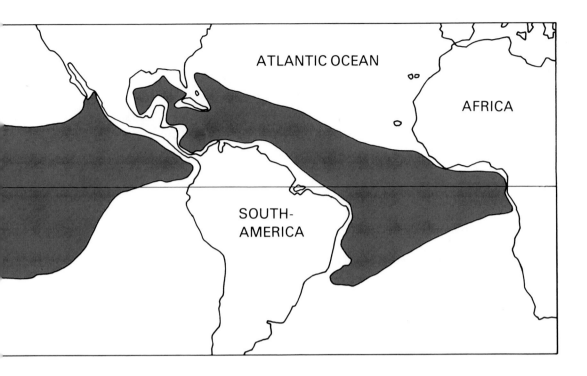

among the fuels that can be obtained.

Garbage, as we know only too well, is a fast-growing commodity, its growth keeping pace with the growth of urban populations and of affluence. But the growth rate of biomass in the ocean surpasses anything we know on land. The green alga *Chlorella*, for instance, grows exponentially. It multiplies itself by four in the space of 24 hours. One *Chlorella* becomes sixteen on the third day, sixty-four on the fourth. In theory, it could continue to multiply until it achieved about the same weight as the earth. This, of course, is only theory. In practice *Chlorella* is unable to get enough sunlight for the photosynthetic activity that powers its expansion. Despite this, its growth rate is stunning. A plant of giant kelp, on the other hand, grows at the rate of 3 meters a day: you can almost see it grow!

Energy crops on land compete with food crops for dwindling agricultural space. The space for energy crops in the oceans is practically unlimited. While at first sight it may

strike the reader as science fiction or fantasy to think in terms of a 124,000-acre ocean energy farm, this kind of proposal, made by serious scientists and industrial planners, becomes plausible once our minds adjust to the different dimensions of the ocean world.

The most ambitious project of this kind is the Ocean Food and Energy Farm, projected, planned, and realized on an experimental basis by Dr. Howard Wilcox of San Diego and sponsored by the US Navy and various private companies. After an initial phase, during which a 7-acre experimental farm was developed, the plan provides for expansion, over several years, into a 99,000-acre farm, at an overall cost of $1.9 billion (1976). According to the detailed systems design made for this ambitious project, such a farm could yield enough food for about 750,000 people and enough energy and other products to support more than 47,000 people at today's US per capita consumption levels, or up to 300,000 at today's world average per capita consumption levels. The farm prod-

Handling an RCM 5 current meter. A navigation
disk buoy is visible on the left.

20. Schematic of closed-cycle OTEC system

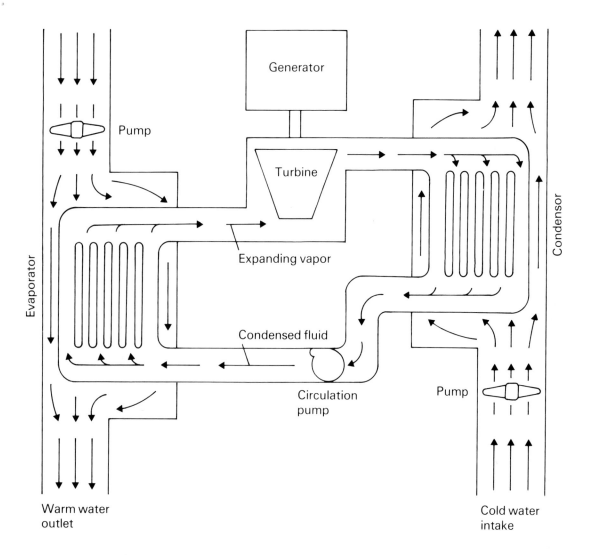

Generator

Pump

Turbine

Expanding vapor

Evaporator

Condensed fluid

Condensor

Circulation pump

Pump

Warm water outlet

Cold water intake

ucts, according to the design, would consist of feed for fish and livestock as well as food for human beings, methane gas, fertilizers, ethanol, lubricants, waxes, plastic, fiber—a complete spectrum of useful petrochemical-type products.

Yet another form of ocean energy generation called Ocean Thermal Energy Conversion, or OTEC for short, has reached the most advanced stage of research and development.

A Mini-OTEC plant has been constructed off the coast of Hawaii. It was developed by a consortium which included the University of Hawaii, Lockheed Missiles and

Space Company, Dillingham Construction and Dredging Company, and Alfa-Laval. Its performance surpassed the most optimistic hopes and expectations. The Mini-OTEC plant produces a net energy output of 50 kilowatts.

Based on this experience, a Pilot Plant, able to produce as much as 10 to 40 megawatts, was planned. This was to be followed by a commercial-size plant capable of generating 400 megawatts, or about half as much as a small nuclear power station. But financial problems arose, and Lockheed withdrew from the project.

Two new consortia, General Electric and Ocean Thermoresources, took over the project. Funded by the US federal government, the new five-year plan foresees a commercial-size plant, with a net output of 40 megawatts per year, by 1987. This power would be fed into Hawaii's electric power grid.

OTEC, pioneered by the French engineers Georges Claude and P. Boucheret three-quarters of a century ago, is based on a simple principle: the utilization of the difference between the higher temperatures of the surface water and the lower temperatures of the deeper waters. In tropical seas, this difference amounts to about 20° to 25°C.

The warm water, which can be further heated by first passing it through shallow pans (which might also be used for aquaculture) or through solar panels, is used to generate low-pressure steam that is passed through a turbine generating electricity. The cold water is used to condense the vapor into liquid. The liquid used for evaporation may be either ammonium (anhydrous ammonia) or sea water. Ammonium has the advantage that it evaporates at lower temperatures. After recondensation it is returned to the evaporator, and the cycle is repeated in a closed system. If sea water is used instead, the condensate is distilled water, drinking water thus becoming a by-product of this process. This method appears to be far simpler and requires no heat exchangers, but a great deal more work remains to be done. Very large amounts of cold water are required for this

process: to produce energy on a commercial scale, 3,000 cubic meters per second would have to be pumped up from a depth of at least 900 meters. Add to this a similar volume of warm surface water required for the evaporation process, and the total pumping rate is about equal to the flow rate of the river Nile!

There are a number of basic designs for OTEC plants (Figures 20 and 21). They vary according to the use to which the energy generated is to be put. One type of plant is a permanent structure, moored near shore, with the electricity generated being transmitted to a power grid for distribution on land. This is possible only where continental shelves are narrow, slopes are steep, and the water is deep near shore—otherwise power transmission by cable causes economic and technical difficulties. The size and shape of the platform are not too different from those of the oil production platforms now in use, for instance in the North Sea. The weight of these platforms is somewhat above half a million metric tons!

Another design links the OTEC plant to a large "plant ship" for direct use by an energy-intensive industry, such as metal or mineral processing or ammonia production. Such plants can be mobile. They could, for example, follow a nodule-mining or mud-mining ship, providing energy for mining and for processing at sea. They could also cruise around tropical seas in search of spots where the temperature differences are greatest ("grazing" plants).

The recently discovered hot-water vents along the mid-oceanic ridges open yet another perspective. Instead of pumping up cold water from the bottom and bringing it into contact with warmer surface water, a method by which a temperature differential of at most 20° to 25°C can be obtained, one could pump up hot bottom water and bring it into contact with cool surface water, with a temperature differential of at least 300°C! Alex Malahoff, one of the discoverers of the hot-water vents along the Galapagos Ridge, suggests that the energy potential of these

21. Schematic of open-cycle OTEC system

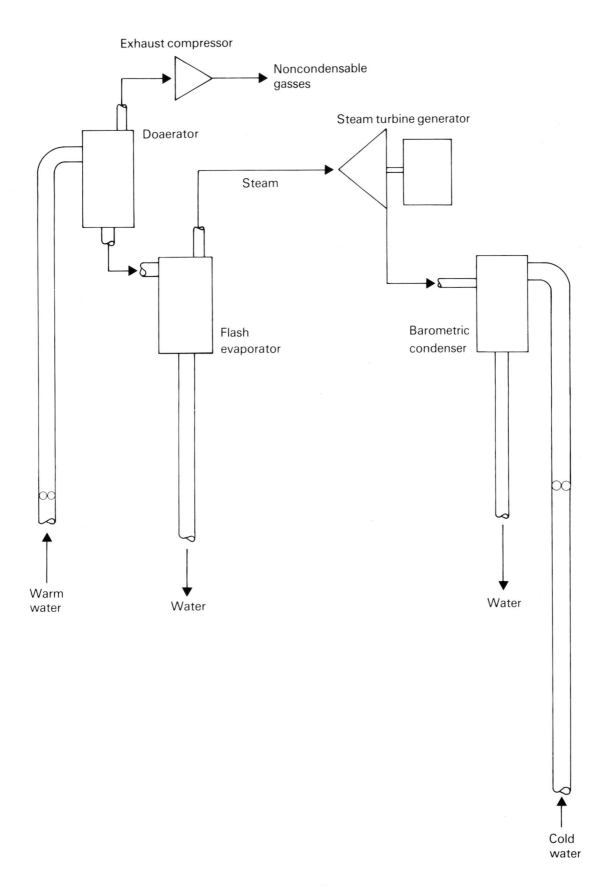

Exhaust compressor

Noncondensable gasses

Doaerator

Steam turbine generator

Steam

Flash evaporator

Barometric condenser

Warm water

Water

Water

Cold water

hydrothermal phenomena may be of even greater economic interest than the associated minerals and metals.

Substantial work remains to be done on surface platform design, mooring systems, heat exchangers, pipes, prevention of fouling, and economical power distribution, but the potential for applying ocean energy to ocean mining is obviously enormous. Neptune's forges call for Neptune's fires.

The most stunning energy potential in the oceans, surprisingly, is that of salinity gradients. Only recently taken seriously by marine technologists, this method of extracting energy from the sea is based, like OTEC, on a very simple scientific principle: exploiting the osmotic pressure generated by the contact between less salty and more salty water. In their study, Isaacs and Schmitt have calculated that the salinity energy density of a river with respect to the sea is equivalent to the energy density of a 2,400-meter dam. "Where large rivers flow into the sea, salinity gradient energy is renewable and its utilization at very low efficiencies is defensible—in the Congo, for instance, the full power released in dilution is about 10^5 (100,000) MW"!

Sea water with respect to a coastal brine pond is equivalent to a dam 3,500 meters high. "In terms of power, freshwater or seawater flowing into brine at the rate of 1 m per second releases energy at the rate of 30 MW" . . . and "salt domes in coastal regions, which are common traps for petroleum, have two or three orders of magnitude more energy in the form of latent salinity power than in the oil they might contain"!

The figures are truly staggering. "Only the natural fluxes of salinity and temperature gradients could provide energy in excess of the estimated 21st century levels of electric power consumption," Isaacs and Schmitt conclude.

While the potential of salinity gradients is at present more theoretical than practical, various technological means have already been proposed to realize it. Some of them require membranes for the osmotic exchange, and membranes entail problems of a technical nature, of cost, and of durability. In the Arctic or Antarctic regions, it has been suggested, sea water or brine water at a temperature below the freezing point of fresh water could be used to freeze fresh water in pressure vessels. The pressure of the expanding ice, during freezing, is used to produce power. "In addition, any of the various schemes for desalination of seawater that have received attention in the last two decades and that are fundamentally reversible, are potential processes for the extraction of energy by salination."

As we try to adjust our thinking to the different dimensions of the ocean world, we must make a second adjustment: we must think in an integrated and integrative way. Resources can no longer be considered as something "given" in determined quantities. Resources, energy (including labor), time, and technology are linked in one equation, the key variable being technology. In this context, and applying a different scale to energy and time, the masses of diffused and eternally renewable minerals and metals in the oceans become resources: they can be exploited and used. To consider resources in this integrated, dynamic context must profoundly affect our concepts of property and ownership. When one thinks of a rock, or a piece of gold, as something circumscribed and finite, one can pretend to own it. But one cannot own in the same sense a process that is open-ended and infinite, a process that transcends individuals or nations.

Thinking in this integrated way we can also see that the product is as complex as the process. Ocean energy technologies typically do not serve the single purpose of generating electricity. They become more effective, and more economical, the more purposes they are allowed to serve simultaneously. Thus we have seen that salinity-gradient power generation is related to processes of desalination. Desalination, furthermore, becomes more economical if the residual brines, or bitterns, can be further mined for additional minerals, such as potassium and magnesium.

Likewise, thermal gradient power can produce distilled, desalinated drinking water; and it can produce ammonia. Considering its association with artificial upwellings (the pumping of cold bottom water to the surface) and with shallow sun-heated pans or basins, it may be linked with various forms of aquaculture, thereby enhancing food production. It can also be directly applied to air-conditioning by forcing the cold water through a spray-chamber in a driven flow of air. This method, applicable along tropical coasts bordering steep continental shelves where OTEC can be used, is infinitely more effective than traditional air-conditioning. The same amount of electric energy required to air-condition one unit with traditional methods now suffices to air-condition 2,000 such units!

While capturing the tides for the generation of electricity, the same tidal flow can also be utilized to dredge harbors and harbor channels, work that is at present very energy-intensive. The extraction of energy from biomass can be combined with genetic engineering of the biomass itself. Special strains of marine plants might be cultivated with an enhanced capacity for concentrating heavy metals. This capacity might, in turn, be used for the simultaneous purposes of eliminating a pollutant and "mining" a metal. The efficient multipurpose application of ocean energy-generation processes requires new management practices and horizontal integration of existing industrial and governmental infrastructures. No sector of activities can stand alone in the ocean world. They all interact.

The shift from predominantly land-based to predominantly sea-based energy resources and technologies is part of the ongoing penetration of the industrial revolution into the oceans; it is part of what we have called the marine revolution. This revolution will have social, anthropological, even evolutionary consequences which we are only just beginning to fathom.

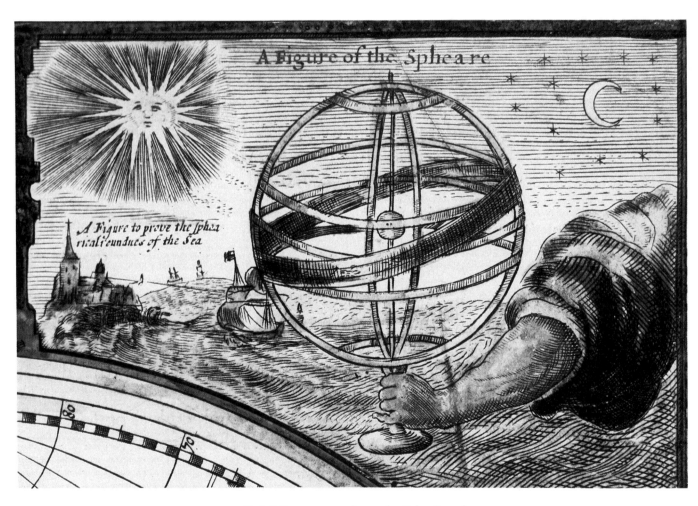

Detail from a map drawn by John Speed,
published in *A Prospect of the most Famous Ports of
the World*, London, 1676.

∭ Chapter 6 ∭
THE COMMON HERITAGE OF MANKIND

The mines of Neptune are a challenge to humankind in more than one sense. Their wealth is, for all practical purposes, boundless. The technological challenge of ocean mining is enormous—comparable only to, and related to, that of the conquest of outer space. While we are just beginning to understand life around us—our kind of life, and the minds of our fellow creatures—we know nothing as yet about the mind of the deep, and life in the oceanic abysses is as alien to us as that of another planet. But we do know that the ocean environment is fragile, that we may alter it as we conquer it, and that changes in the ocean environment may affect our own lives in ways we cannot predict. The ecological challenge inherent in assessing, and preventing, the consequences of applying the new technologies to the exploitation of the mines of Neptune is equally enormous.

To this we must add the fact that the rules of law, the standards and concepts developed for mining on land do not fit and cannot work for the oceans. As we have seen, the wealth of the oceans eludes the terrestrial concepts of boundaries and ownership and requires new systems of management and law. The legal and philosophical challenges inherent in the penetration of ocean space by the industrial revolution are as enormous as the technological and ecological challenges.

All this was brought to the attention of the world community in a historic three-hour address delivered by Dr. Arvid Pardo, ambassador of Malta, before the General Assembly of the United Nations on November 1, 1967. He proposed that the mineral wealth of the oceans be declared by the United Nations to be the common heritage of mankind, and as such, that it could not be appropriated by any nation, individual, or company; that this wealth be managed on behalf of all countries for the benefit of mankind as a whole; that it be used for peaceful purposes only; and that resources and ocean environment be used with caution, to be preserved for future generations.

This was a totally revolutionary concept. Coming at a time when the old law of the sea had been eroded by expanding national claims and the intensification and transformation of ocean uses, the Maltese proposal set off a chain reaction of events in the United Nations and other international forums, leading eventually to the calling of the Third United Nations Conference on the Law of the Sea (1973–1982), the largest, longest, and most comprehensive international conference ever held.

As negotiations went on, it became clear that "the problems of ocean space are closely interrelated and need be considered as a whole," that the new order established for the oceans implied a new international order for the world community in general, that the Convention on the Law of the Sea, probably the most ambitious document ever attempted, was really a "Constitution for the

Oceans" and potentially a model for, or nucleus of, a Constitution for the World. Neptune's trident is the scepter of the world, an old saying goes.

The International Seabed Authority, charged with responsibility for the management of the common heritage of mankind, was the heart of this constitution. The Seabed Authority—in the tradition of other international organizations—was to consist of an assembly for setting general policy, an executive council with its specialized commissions, and a secretariat. But in addition, the Authority was to have an operational arm, the "Enterprise," through which it could engage directly in mining activities on behalf of the world community as a whole. This would have generated revenue which could have been utilized for research, for the conservation of the ocean environment, and for development purposes. The whole institution, finally, was linked to a general system for the peaceful settlement of disputes regarding ocean activities.

Here was a prototype of the first public international resource-management institution. Here was a first agreement establishing a structured relationship between multinational companies and a public international institution. Here was a first acceptance of the principle of international taxation. Here was the framework for an international environmental law, for international surveillance and enforcement, for law that was binding on states and persons. Here was a new, dynamic concept of ownership and sovereignty, embodied in the principle of the common heritage: more functional, more in harmony with the environmental and technological conditions of our age than are the static concepts of the past.

All this was enshrined in a Draft Convention on the Law of the Sea, consisting of 320 Articles plus 9 technical Annexes. It was adopted by the Third United Nations Conference on the Law of the Sea in April 1982, with 130 states voting in favor, 4 against, and 17 abstaining. Since then, 143 states have signed the Convention. Whatever the future

may hold, this was a unique achievement.

Inevitably, perspectives and perceptions kept changing over those long years, and indeed, they continue to do so. Compromises were struck; "package deals" were negotiated, and the final product is not what the dreams and hopes of 1967 foretold. This was unavoidable.

The difficulties of establishing in the real world an institution as visionary as the Seabed Authority can easily be imagined. Fundamental conflicts of interest arose between industrialized countries and developing countries, overlaid by, and overlapping with, conflicts between mineral-producing and mineral-consuming states, with either one of these latter groups consisting of both developing and developed countries.

In the context of the dichotomy between developed and developing countries, the developing countries wanted to maximize benefits from the newly created wealth of the oceans. They wanted to make sure of their full participation in the exploitation of the common heritage of mankind, and for that purpose, they wanted a strong and operational Seabed Authority, in whose decision-making they would have a voice proportionate to their numerical strength (about 110 of the roughly 150 member states of the United Nations are developing countries). The developed countries, on the other hand, insisted on free access to the resources which were declared to be the common heritage of mankind; they preferred business as usual, based on advantages which their superior technological and financial infrastructures guaranteed them. They insisted on minimizing the powers and functions of the Seabed Authority so as to prevent it from interfering in this freedom and curtailing these advantages. They kept insisting that every administrative and financial detail be fixed in advance for twenty-five years, unalterably inscribed in the Convention—and this for an industry which, they admitted themselves, was new, untried, and experimental, and whose success, impact, needs, and developments nobody could really predict. The paradox is obvious. It vitiated negotiations, generating a text that grew more complex, more abstruse, more remote from reality with every year that passed.

In the context of the dichotomy between consumer and producer countries, consumer countries were interested in increasing supplies and decreasing prices, while producer countries wanted to make sure that seabed resources should not be allowed to compete with traditional land-based resources. They insisted on production limitation, again to be fixed in advance, in accordance with mathematical formulae which were accepted only when they had become so complicated that no one really understood them, and which, in the final analysis, would not have served the interests of the developing producer countries. The whole argument, furthermore, was based on the illusory assumption that the Authority had a monopoly on the production of nodules, which are found only in the oceanic abysses, in zones which lie, according to any criterion, beyond the limits of national jurisdiction. Therefore, so the reasoning went, the Authority, once established, could enforce its conditions on management and financial arrangements as well as on production limitation on reluctant companies or states.

The reality of the 1980s, however, is different from the picture painted in the '70s. Pressures for internationalization created counterpressures for the assertion of wider national claims. In 1980, unilateral legislation was enacted by the United States and West Germany—to be followed by other states— authorizing their companies to mine the ocean floor underlying the high seas on the basis of domestic law. By 1980 it had also become clear that manganese nodules could and would be mined in areas under national jurisdiction, under bilateral agreements between mining companies and coastal states, such as Mexico, Chile, probably Ecuador, French Polynesia, and others. This meant that the monopoly of the Authority was broken. The Authority now had to compete for contracts with states, and if the general con-

ditions it offered were less favorable, it would be out of business, and that was all there was to it.

Whether the Convention is ratified or not, the role of the International Seabed Authority must be re-examined in the light of this new reality. If it turns out to be useless and cumbersome, it will not be utilized in practice. A paper tiger, it will be bypassed by history and economic reality. A splendid opportunity to create something new and different, a prototype for industrial cooperation between North and South, East and West, a model for international organization in the future, a great dream, a great inspiration, will be lost.

This need not be so. Even within the terms of the Convention, the functions and the structure of the International Seabed Authority can be adapted and adjusted to the changed reality. In spite of the divergence of interests and the conflict of pressure groups, there is a sufficient basis of common interest in and around the exciting new activity of ocean mining. Even in the changed setting, the International Seabed Authority could become a model for international organization. At the present stage of development, the Authority could fulfill four vitally important functions, and the Preparatory Commission established by the United Nations Conference on the Law of the Sea to prepare it for its role in the 1980s and '90s should realistically channel its action in these directions.

The first is cooperative research and development. As we saw in Chapter 3, in the late 1970s the major consortia successfully completed the first phase of their research and development with pilot mining tests which clearly demonstrated that manganese nodule mining is technically feasible. This phase of research and development was costly. About $200 million was invested by the major companies, and this, considering the high risks involved, triggered the absorption of the private sector into huge, globe-spanning consortia: complex commercial organizations in which national companies first formed a sort of federation, and a number of such federations then merged in a multinational consortium. A federation of federations of industries was created.

The second phase of research and development, during which pilot operations will have to be scaled up to commercial dimensions, will require about three times the investment made during the first phase. One single, fully developed commercial enterprise producing about 3 million tons of nodules a year may cost as much as $1 to $1.5 billion.

These are not absurdly high figures for the mining industry, but there are factors that make it unlikely that private industry will rush into this kind of investment at this time. We are moving through a depression. Low and unstable metal prices, oversupplies of land-based resources, investments already directed toward traditional land-based sources, make it extremely difficult for a pioneering high-risk industry to get off the ground. In fact, consortia are already in the process of disbanding, and the further development of deep-sea mining technology is being placed "on the back burner."

And yet everyone agrees that deep-sea minerals and metals are needed: not now perhaps, but in ten to fifteen years most certainly. To reassemble the dismantled machinery, however, will take at least ten years after the new start. In other words, much valuable effort and a great deal of money will have been wasted.

Industry is aware of all this. If the collaboration of governments were forthcoming, industry might be prepared to go ahead. This is the case in Japan, but it is not the case in the other industrialized countries, where other priorities may make it difficult to subsidize seabed mining companies. If governments cannot do this individually, however, they might instead be able to do it jointly. Just as the first phase of research and development in seabed mining called for the internationalization of the private sector, the second, more costly, phase calls for the internationalization of the public sector and its

integration with the private sector. This has already happened for the mining of the metalliferous muds in the Red Sea and it should happen for the mining of nodules in the Pacific and Indian oceans. The reasons for the merger are the same as in the case of the private sector: reduction of costs and the spreading of risks. It is the only way to go.

According to the Convention, the International Seabed Authority has the mandate to coordinate and encourage international cooperation in industrial research with regard to seabed mining. It has the right to undertake such research itself, and it has the right to form joint ventures. The first task of the International Seabed Authority in the present world situation, therefore, should be to form a joint venture for research and development, for the phase of scaling up production from the pilot-test level to full commercialized levels; for the establishment of a pilot processing plant, and for an economic feasibility study. Partners in this joint venture should be the Authority and any state or company that wished to participate.

There is at least one interesting precedent for international public/private cooperation and integration in an area of advanced scientific industrial research and development. In 1980 the European Commission put forward a proposal for a five-year Community program of research and development in biomolecular engineering. Biomolecular engineering—the modification and utilization of biological systems (bacteria, enzymes, algae) for industrial purposes—is one of the new developments revolutionizing the industrial system.

The program of the European Community originally covered six subjects, two in the field of enzyme engineering and four in the field of genetic engineering. What is of particular interest for the Seabed Authority is the way in which these programs are financed. The European Community puts up part of the money and national governments the remainder, through cost-sharing contracts between the Commission and private or public organizations in the member states. Each project is to be controlled by a small research group.

The total cost over five years was to be 49 million European units of account (approximately $62 million), of which 26 million European units of account would come from Community funds. In other words, about 53 percent of the investment was to be borne by the Community, and 47 percent was to be contributed by states and their industrial companies.

During the course of negotiations, the program was somewhat scaled down. The compromise proposal included an allocation of funds for training and education in the areas covered by five of the six projects in the program. The program of research and development, on the other hand, was reduced from six projects to three, and the total cost to the Commission was cut from 26 million to 11.8 million European units of account, which amounts to about $15 million over four and a half years.

Obviously the scale of this project is much smaller. A research and development program for seabed mining might run to $600 million. Seabed mining is a capital-intensive industry, and the stage of R & D is more advanced—all the more reason for proceeding on a cooperative basis. The format, nevertheless, might be the same as that provided by the European Community for R & D in bioengineering. As was pointed out in a recent debate in the British House of Lords, when the European program was debated: "There is a general disposition to support a constructive community action in the field of advanced technology."

At the Versailles summit held in June 1982, President Mitterrand of France proposed the launching of a "concerted program" establishing "international commissions for research and development and for technological cooperation between private firms, the public sector and States" in various fields of advanced technology, among which he explicitly mentioned "ocean explo-

ration." In this proposal he stressed the importance of the participation of developing countries in joint ventures to assure them access to these technologies.

Nothing could be more in line with the French proposal than the suggestion that the International Seabed Authority, and the Commission established to prepare its activities, should concentrate their early efforts on establishing a joint venture or joint ventures for exploration and research and development in ocean mining.

Cooperation of this kind, obviously, can be carried out regardless of boundaries between national and international geographic areas, as demonstrated by the European precedent. Nor does it prejudice the way in which commercial exploitation is subsequently to be organized: whether internationally or bilaterally or nationally. If the experiment in international R & D was successful, however, it is likely that the chances of continuing with a joint venture system for the phases of exploitation and processing would be greater than they are today. A joint venture in international R & D would be a great learning experience for everyone concerned.

The advantages for the industrialized mining states would be considerable. They would be supporting their ailing mining industries, with likely spin-offs for other industries, and they would maintain continuity in preparing for commercial production when needed. They would utilize and develop their technologies and enhance international trade in their technologies. What is more, smaller industrial states which otherwise would have no chance to participate in the development of seabed mining could become partners in the joint venture.

Developing countries, on the other hand, would be represented on the Authority's side of the venture and would benefit from technology transfers to the Authority and from participation in the management of a scientific/technological enterprise with likely spin-offs for their internal development. Countries like Chile, Ecuador, and

Mexico, which intend to exploit nodules in areas under their national jurisdiction, would probably be the first ones to want to join such a venture. But seabed technology holds promises for other developing countries too. Far from being esoteric and of interest to only a few highly industrialized countries, seabed technology includes an array of auxiliary technologies which, disaggregated, are directly and immediately useful to developing countries: in the sectors of petroleum and mineral exploration and exploitation, of ship construction and navigation, and of a whole series of oceanographic sciences and skills directly applicable to the management of exclusive economic zones.

Research and development, furthermore, need not and should not be restricted to manganese nodule mining. Just like the European Community, the Seabed Authority could organize more than one project of R & D in advanced industrial technologies. A most suitable candidate, for example, would be energy generation from the oceans, with special emphasis on OTEC and salinity gradient energy conversion, which could appropriately be pioneered by the International Seabed Authority. This, however, may be a few years in the future, although it certainly is not too soon to begin to think about it.

Thus, the first useful function of the International Seabed Authority in the 1980s would be the establishment of joint ventures in research and development.

The second function, related to the first, would be for the Seabed Authority to assist developing countries in exploring their continental shelves and the economic zones under their jurisdiction. Such a function is not foreseen in the Convention although it is in no way prohibited by it. The requirement must be that the states wish the Authority to engage in the activity.

Most underdeveloped countries are underexplored. No one knows how much oil there is. There may not be the kind of giant fields that would be profitable to the big oil companies, but there might be enough to al-

leviate growing oil import bills. At present, there is no one around to do the job. The Report of the Brandt Commission points out that in the past few years as much as 80 to 90 percent of the spending on exploration has been concentrated in a very few of the developed or newly industrialized countries, whereas it has almost entirely ceased in large areas of the Third World. "Here, therefore," the report continues, "is an area where new initiatives, involving imaginative new arrangements, can clearly be in the interest of North and South alike. Measures are needed to speed up exploration and exploitation of deposits in developing countries, while assuring a full share of the benefits of mining, processing and exportation to the host country government." The Brandt Commission Report recommends international action to assist development in the exploration of these mineral resources.

The Government of Canada responded to this recommendation by establishing Petrocanada International to perform this service. Petrocanada is a subsidiary of the commercial Crown Corporation Petrocanada, whose technology and know-how it shares. It is financed independently, however, through allocations from Parliament. About half a billion dollars have been allocated for the first four years of operation. These funds are not to be recovered. Petrocanada International is an instrument of Canada's policy of development cooperation.

While this is a splendid beginning, it is obvious that one country alone could not, and should not, attempt to fill the need on a global basis. Clearly, a public international institution is needed to coordinate services of the kind offered by Canada and now supported by Mexico and Venezuela. There is no need to create a new institution with a new bureaucracy. No institution can be more suited than the International Seabed Authority with its enterprise system, its technology, and its possibilities of matching funds provided by states and their companies with public international funds. Here again, the

International Seabed Authority could respond to an immediate need, through "imaginative new arrangements" already preformed in the Law of the Sea Convention. All that is needed is the political will to utilize this potential by interpretation and state practice.

The third practical function of the Seabed Authority in the 1980s and '90s could be to ensure that at least one sector of ocean space, that is, the seabed and ocean floor and "the subsoil thereof" beyond the limits of national jurisdiction, should be exempt from the arms race and preserved for peaceful purposes only.

In 1970 the United Nations General Assembly adopted a Treaty Prohibiting the Emplacement of Atomic Weapons and Other Weapons of Mass Destruction in the Seabed and Ocean Floor and in the Subsoil Thereof, one of the deplorably few instances where disarmament efforts led to any positive conclusions at all. The treaty, however, suffers from a number of weaknesses. The weakest point, perhaps, is that there are no adequate provisions for surveillance and enforcement. The treaty stipulated that each state party to the treaty was to have the right to verify through observation the seabed activities of all parties. But this was difficult to accept for states that did not possess the requisite technologies for such inspection. During the negotiations that led to adoption of the treaty, the majority of states pressed for the internationalization of controls. A number of proposals were put forward. Some delegations wanted a special body responsible for surveilling seabed installations and monitoring compliance with the prohibitions of the treaty. Others suggested that existing international organizations could be entrusted with the task. Canada proposed that the Secretary-General of the United Nations be given a major role in controlling verification procedures. Both the USA and the USSR objected to the internationalization of verification procedures. They considered it unnecessary, premature, and costly to establish a special body

and equip it with the necessary technology. The Seabed Authority did not exist at that time, and nobody could predict the form that it would eventually take.

Now the situation is entirely different. The Seabed Authority is ideally prepared to assume this function. If it is to engage in geophysical exploration, it must have the seismic and sonar technologies required for exploration. The same technologies could be employed for surveillance and for monitoring any activity on the seabed.

The Seabed Authority is also equipped with the organizational machinery for monitoring and surveillance. The Convention provides for a Technical Commission, with a "staff of inspectors . . . who shall inspect activities in the area to determine whether the provisions of the Convention are carried out faithfully." On the request of any state party or other concerned party, the members of the commission and their staff of inspectors are to be accompanied by a representative of the state or other party making the request when carrying out this function of supervision and inspection. Again, all that is needed is the political will to utilize this machinery and the technology, in this case for both the enhancement of disarmament and development of the seabed.

The Seabed Disarmament Treaty is due for review and revision every five years. At the next review conference, member states might decide to amend the article entrusting verification to states only. In addition, they might assign this function to the Authority. Any state party might then request that its representative should accompany the inspectorate on its surveillance missions. Smaller states and developing countries that have so far been unable to share in this activity would thus be given the possibility to do so.

What may have been premature and costly in 1970 thus becomes practical and functional in the 1980s. While enhancing the role of the International Seabed Authority as an instrument of international industrial cooperation, an important precedent would be set for international monitoring and surveillance of disarmament agreements. A complementary proposal has already been made for outer space: in 1979 the government of France proposed the establishment of an international satellite agency to monitor disarmament agreements from outer space.

The fourth crucially important function of the International Seabed Authority would be the protection and conservation of the marine environment on the deep-sea floor. This, too, is already foreseen in the Convention on the Law of the Sea, but its provisions must be interpreted and developed. The Authority indeed has the responsibility for "the protection and conservation of the natural resources of the Area and the prevention of damage to the flora and fauna of the marine environment." For this purpose it also has the right to "issue emergency orders, which may include orders for the suspension or adjustment of operations, to prevent serious harm to the marine environment arising out of any activity in the Area," and to "disapprove areas for exploitation by contractors or the Enterprise in cases where substantial evidence indicates the risk of serious harm to the marine environment." This, certainly, provides an excellent springboard for action.

But emergency measures are apt to come too late. The effects of collision between the different time scales of two different worlds—the multimillion-years ecosystem of the abyssal ocean floor and the fast-moving industrial systems of our age—may be irreversible. We know so little as yet about the world at the bottom of the ocean. And from where is the Authority to gather its "substantial evidence"? What is it to do with the areas "disapproved for exploitation"? Clearly, studies should be undertaken at once to identify the areas that should be "disapproved."

Some of the zones, such as those where plate separation and rifting give rise to hydrothermal vents with their unique flora and fauna, should be designated International Marine Parks. There, the Book of Job says,

Leviathan makes the water at the bottom of the sea boil, and gigantic worms live on the seabed. . . . How did the author of the Book of Job know about these things? We, today, do not know much more about them than he did. But we know that they really do exist, and we do not want to see them destroyed before we know more about them.

The Seabed Authority should administer these seafloor marine parks just as a department for national parks administers the national parks on land and offshore within the jurisdiction of a state.

This suggestion, more timely than ever, is not new. As early as 1971, the provident Maltese government proposed to the United Nations a draft convention in which the International Ocean-Space Institutions would have the mandate to "approve the establishment of scientific stations, nature parks or marine preserves in International Ocean Space." It is an idea whose time has come.

On the basis of research that should be undertaken as a matter of great urgency aimed at establishing just where and how large these marine parks would have to be to fulfill their purpose, the Preparatory Commission could begin at once to prepare the necessary rules and regulations for their administration by the Authority and to organize scientific research on the mysterious forms of life they contain.

An International Seabed Authority, thus reconceptualized and adapted to the changed circumstances of the 1980s and '90s, could simultaneously serve the purposes of industrial development, disarmament, and the protection of the environment in ways which safeguard the interests of North and South and West and East. It would integrate all aspects of ocean mining and thus play a much more significant role in world economics than an institution restricted, not literally (the Convention speaks of the mineral resources of the area in general as the common heritage of mankind) but practically, to manganese nodule mining. It would set a new pattern for international organization.

The mines of Neptune thus promise far more than metals and minerals. The key to the mines is also the key to new ways of looking at our world. To new views and perspectives of the physical world, as it appears in the dreamscapes of oversize mountains and valleys on the ocean floor. To a new understanding of the biological world, embodied in the fantastic, seemingly extraterrestrial living forms found around the hydrothermal vents along the mid-oceanic rifts. To new concepts of the economic world where "resources" become defined in terms of human genius, technology, and aspiration. To the spiritual world and the world of ideals and ideas, where the unique experience of the making of the new law of the sea may help to hasten the transformation of an outworn social, political, and international order.

That transformations of this magnitude are not without dangers goes without saying. But humankind's creative power is as great as its destructive power, to turn a pessimistic saying into an optimistic one. The mines of Neptune present new challenges to our technological, organizational, and philosophical imagination, new hopes for a better, more peaceful, and prosperous world.

Pacem in Maribus

∭ Bibliography ∭

AGARWAL, J. C. et al. "Processing of Ocean Nodules." Paper presented at the 104th Annual Meeting of the AIME. New York, 1975 (mimeo).

AGRICOLA, GEORGIUS. *De res Metallica*. Translated by Herbert Clark Hoover and Lon Henry Hoover. New York: Dover Publications, 1950.

ALESCO (Arab League Educational and Scientific Organisation). *Programme for Environmental Studies in the Red Sea and Gulf of Aden.* Jeddah II Conference, January 1976, Provisional Report.

AMANN, HANS. "Erdöl aus der Tiefsee." *Techniken der Zukunft*, no. 8 (1974): 40–44.

BÄCKER, HARALD. "Mineral Resources in Coastal Areas." Inter-regional Seminar on Development and Management of Resources of Coastal Areas. West Berlin, Hamburg, Kiel and Cuxhaven, May 31–June 14, 1976. Proceedings, 291–300.

BÄCKER, HARALD, with contributions from HANS ALBERT ROESER, MARTIN HARTMANN, and BERNHARD MATTIAT. "Erzschlämme." *Geologisches Jahrbuch*, Series D, no. 38 (1980): 77–108.

BÄCKER, HARALD, and JOHANNES POST. "Study of Ore Sludges in the Red Sea." *Meerestechnik* 9, no. 4 (August 1978): 109–44.

BÄCKER, HARALD, and M. SCHOELL. "New Deeps with Brines and Metalliferous Sediments in the Red Sea." *Nature*, no. 140 (1972): 153–58.

BACKHURST, J. R., and J. H. HARKER. *Process Plant Design*. New York: Elsevier, 1973.

BARR, D. I. H. "Power from the Tides and Waves." In *The Marine Environment*. Edited by John Lenihan and William W. Fletcher. Vol. 5. New York/San Francisco: Academic Press, 1977.

BATURNI, G. N., and P. L. BEYRUKOV. "Phosphorites on the Sea Floor and their Origin." *Marine Geology* 31 (1979): 317–32.

BLISSENBACH, E. "Prospective Sedimental Mineral Potentials of the South American Atlantic Margin." *Memorias del Seminario Sobre Ecologia Bentonica y Sedimentacion de la Plataforme Continental del Atlantico Sur.* Montevideo, Agosto 1979: 383–403.

CAMERON, HUGH, GLYN FORD, et al. *Manganese Nodule Mining: Issues and Perspectives*. Manchester, UK: Policy Research in Engineering, Science and Technology (PREST). February 1980.

CHARLIER, ROGER. *Harnessing the Energies of the Oceans: A Review and Bibliography.* Washington, D.C.: Marine Technological Society. No date.

COUNCIL ON ENVIRONMENTAL QUALITY. *North Sea Oil and Gas: Implications for Future United States Development*. Norman: University of Oklahoma Press, 1973.

CRONAN, D. S. "Riches of the Ocean Floor." In *Oceanography: Contemporary Readings in Ocean Science*, 2nd ed. Edited by R. G. Pirie. New York: Oxford University Press, 1977.

CRUICKCHANK, M. J. *Marine Mining: SME Mining Engineering Handbook*. New York: Society of Mining Engineers, 1973.

DAMES and MOORE, and EIC CORPORATION. *Description of Manganese Nodule Processing Activities for Environmental Studies*. 2 vols. Rockville, Md.: U.S. Department of Commerce, NOAA, Office of Marine Minerals, 1977.

_____, and BENJAMIN V. ANDREWS. *Draft Report: A Description of Transportation and Waste Disposal Systems for Manganese Nodule Processing*. Rockville, Md.: U.S. Department of Commerce, NOAA, Office of Marine Minerals, 1977.

DIETZ, R. S. "Mineral Resources and Power." In *Exploring the Ocean World. A History of Oceanography.* Edited by C. P. Idyll. New York: Thomas Y. Crowell, 1969.

DOLGOFF, A. "Mineral Resources of the World's Oceans: An Overview." In *Resources of the World's Oceans.* Edited by H. R. Frey. New York: Institute of Ocean Resources, October 1972.

DREVER, JAMES I., ed. *Sea Water: Cycles of the Major Elements*. Benchmark Papers in Geology, Vol. 45. New York: Halstead Press, 1977.

EARNEY, FILLIMORE C. F. *Petroleum and Hard Minerals from the Sea*. London: Edward Arnold, 1980.

EMERY, K. O. et al. "Summary of Hot Brines and Heavy Metal Deposits in the Red Sea." In *Hot Brines and Recent Heavy Metal Deposits in the Red Sea.* Edited by E. T. Degens and D. A. Ross. New York: Springer Verlag, 1969.

FELLERER, R. "Method and Problems of the Exploration of Manganese Nodules." In *Oceanology International '75.* Conference Papers. Brighton, England (16–21 March 1975): 121–26.

FELLERER, R., and F. NEUWEILER. "Technologische Entwicklung im Marinen Bergbau." *Erdöl and Kohle-Erdgas-Petro-chemie Vereinigt mit Brennstoff Chemie* 31, no. 3 (March 1979): 119–27.

GASKELL, THOMAS F. *Physics of the Earth*. London: Thames and Hudson; New York: Funk and Wagnalls, 1970.

GAUTHIER, M., and J. MARVALDI, "The Two-Ship CLB (Continuous Line Buckets) System for Mining Polymetallic Nodules." *Oceanology International '75.* Conference Papers. Brighton, England (16–21 March 1975): 346–49.

GEORGHIOU, LUKE, and GLYN FORD. "Arab Silver from the Red Sea Mud." *New Scientist*, 19 February 1981, 470–72.

GESAMP (Joint Group of Experts on the Scientific Aspects of Marine Pollution). "Scientific Aspects of Pollution Arising from the Exploration and Exploitation of the Sea-Bed." *Reports and Studies*, no. 7, United Nations, 1977.

GLASBY, G. P. "Minerals from the Sea." *Endeavour* (new series) 3, no. 2 (1979): 82–85.

GOODIER, J. L. "How to Mine Marine Minerals." *World Mining* 20, no. 8 (July 1967): 44–47.

GOVETT, G. J. S., and M. H. GOVETT. *World Mineral Supplies*. Amsterdam: Elsevier, 1976.

HABER, FRITZ. "Das Gold im Meerwasser." Berlin-Dahlem: Kaiser Wilhelm Institute für Physikalische Chemie, 19 May 1926. *Zeitschrift für Angewandte Chemie* 4 (1927): 303–14.

HADDON, H. C. "The Scientific Results of the 'Challenger' Expedition." *Nat. Sci, London* 7 (1895): 7–75.

HALKYARD, JOHN E. "Deep Ocean Mining—Current Status and Future Prospects." *Ocean Industry* 14, no. 5 (1979): 49–51.

ISAACS, JOHN D., and WALTER R. SCHMITT. "Ocean Energy: Forms and Prospects." *Science* 207, no. 4428 (18 January 1980): 265–73.

JAENICKE, GUNTHER, ERICH SCHANZE, and WOLFGANG HAUSER. *A Joint Venture Agreement for Seabed Mining*. Frankfurt am Main: Alfred Metzner Verlag, 1981.

KAPLAN, IRVING. "Mater Omnium." In *Tides of Change*. Edited by Elisabeth Mann Borgese and David Krieger. New York: Mason and Charter, 1975.

KARBE, LUDWIG. "The Possible Impact on the Environment from Deep Sea Mining." In *Ocean Mining: An Interdisciplinary Manual*. IOI Occasional Paper No. 7. Malta: International Ocean Institute, 1981.

KAUTILYA. *Arthasastra*. Translated by R. SHAMASASHY, with an introductory note by J. F. FLEET. Mysore: Sri Raghuveer Printing Press, 1956.

KENT, SIR PETER. *Minerals from the Marine Environment*. London: Edward Arnold, 1980.

KRUEGER, ROBERT B. "The Promise of OTEC." *Marine Technology Journal* 14, no. 2 (June 1980): 32–37.

LINEBAUGH, RUTH M. "Ocean Mining in the Soviet Union." *Marine Technology Journal* 14, no. 1 (March 1980): 20–24.

LINKLETTER, E. *The Voyage of the Challenger*. London: John Murray Ltd., 1972.

LONCAREVIC, B. D. "Prospects for Deep-Sea Mining." Address to the First Canadian Science Writers Workshop Symposium, Ottawa, 13–15 January 1972 (mimeo).

MANN BORGESE, ELISABETH. *The Drama of the Oceans*. New York: Harry N. Abrams, 1976.

———. "The Law of the Sea: The Next Phase." *Third World Quarterly* 4, no. 4 (October 1982): 692–718.

———. "The Role of the International Seabed Authority in the 1980s." *San Diego Law Review* 18, no. 3 (1981): 395–407.

MARJORAM, TONY, HUGH CAMERON, GLYN FORD, ANGELA GARDNER, and MICHAEL GIBBONS. "Manganese Nodules and Marine Technology." *Resources Policy* 12, no. 1 (March 1981).

MCKELVEY, V. E. "Seabed Minerals and the Law of the Sea." *Science* 209 (25 July 1980): 464–72.

MCROBIE, JOHN, and DANNY GREEN. *Potash Extraction from the Dead Sea: A Summary*. PREST Occasional Paper No. 5. Manchester: Department of Liberal Studies in Science, Manchester University, 20 June 1980.

MERO, JOHN. *The Marine Resources of the Sea*. Elsevier Oceanography Series. Amsterdam: Elsevier Publishing Co., 1966.

———. "Ocean Mining—An Historical Perspective." *Marine Mining* 1 (1978): 243–55.

MEYER, KURT. "Wirtschaftlich interessante Schwermineral-Anreicherungen vor Moçambique." *Erzmetall* 30, no. 10 (1977): 452–56. Stuttgart: Dr. Riederer Verlag GmbH.

MILES, EDWARD, and JOHN KING GAMBLE. *Law of the Sea: Conference Outcomes and Problems of Implementation*. Cambridge: Ballinger, 1977.

MUSTAFFA, ZAKI (Saudi Arabian-Sudanese Red Sea Joint Commission) and HANS AMANN (Preussag AG). "Ocean Mining and Protection of the Marine Environment in the Red Sea." Paper presented at the Tenth Annual Offshore Technology Conference (OTC), Houston, Texas, 8–11 May 1978. *Proceedings*, Vol. 2, Paper No. 3188, 1199–1214.

NYHART, J. D., Lance Antrim et al. *A Cost Model of Deep Ocean Mining and Associated Regulatory Issues*. Cambridge, Mass.: Massachusetts Institute of Technology. Report Number MITSG 78-4, March 1978.

Ocean Management 7, no. 1 (June 1981). Special Issue: *Oceanology International '80*. "Ocean Mining and Dredging." K. J. Derkmann, R. Fellerer and H. Richter; J.-P. Lenoble; D. R. Denman; 1–25.

RAMNEY, WILLIAM M. *Offshore Oil Technology:*

Recent Developments. New Jersey: Noyes Data Corporation, 1979.

RICHARDS, WILLIAM E., and JOSEPH R. VADUS. "Ocean Thermal Energy Conversion: Technology Development." *Marine Technology Journal* 14, no. 1 (February/March 1980): 3–14.

RICKARD, T. A. *Man and Metal.* New York and London: McGraw-Hill Book Co., 1932.

RIDING, ALAN. "The Mixed Blessings of Mexico's Oil." *The New York Times Magazine,* 11 January 1981, 22–25, 56, 58, 59.

RITCHIE-CALDER, LORD (PETER). *The Pollution of the Mediterranean.* Bern: Herbert Lang, 1972.

ROELS, C. S. "Environmental Impact of Two Manganese Nodule Mining Tests." In *Manganese Nodule Deposits in the Pacific.* Honolulu, 1972, 129–46.

SCHOTT, WOLFGANG. "Mineral (inorganic) Resources of the Oceans and Ocean Floors: A General Review." In *Handbook of Strata-Bound and Stratiform Ore Deposits.* Vol. 3, *Supergene and Surficial Ore Deposits: Textures and Fabrics.* Edited by K. H. Wolf. Amsterdam/Oxford/New York: Elsevier Scientific Publishing Co., 1976.

SEIBOLD, E. "Deepsea Manganese Nodules: The Challenge Since 'Challenger.' " *Episodes,* no. 4 (1978): 3–8.

SID-AHMED, MOHAMED. "Oil on Troubled Societies." *Development Forum* (United Nations Centre for Economic and Social Information) 11, no. 3 (April 1981): 16.

TANGI, MOHAMED. "Discovering Oil in West and Central Africa: A Mixed Blessing." *The Siren: News from UNEP's Regional Seas Programme,* no. 17 (July 1982): 9–16.

Technology Assessment Group Science and Public Policy Program. *Energy Under the Oceans.* Norman: University of Oklahoma Press, 1973.

TINSLEY, C. R. "Manganese-Gains Depend on Recovery in Steel Industry." *Engineering and Mining Journal* 178, no. 3 (1977): 98, 99, 102, 104.

United Nations Conference on Trade and Development (UNCTAD). Report TD/B-721/Add. 1, August 1978.

United Nations Ocean Economics and Technology Branch. *Manganese Nodules: Dimensions and Perspectives,* 1979.

———. *Assessment of Manganese Nodule Resources: Seabed Minerals.* Vol. 1. London: Graham and Trotman, 1982.

United Nations Secretary-General. *Economic Implications of Seabed Mineral Development in the International Area.* Third United Nations Conference on the Law of the Sea, Document A/CONF.62/25, 22 May 1974.

United States Congress, Office of Technology Assessment. *Coastal Effects of Offshore Energy Systems.* OTA-0-37. PB-274 033/06A PCA 13/MF AOI. Washington, D.C., November 1976.

United States Department of Commerce, Office of Ocean Resources and Scientific Policy Coordination. *Cobalt, Copper, Nickel and Manganese: Future Supply and Demand Implications for Deep Seabed Mining.* Rockville, Md. No date.

United States Department of Energy. *Ocean Energy Systems.* Fiscal Year 1979. Program Summary. Springfield, Va.: National Technical Information Service (NTIS). DOE/ET-0118 Dist. Category UC-64.

VON ARX, WILLIAM S. et al. "The Florida Current as a Potential Source of Usable Energy." (mimeo).

WANG, F. F. H., and V. E. MCKELVEY. "Marine Mineral Resources." In *World Mineral Supplies: Assessment and Perspectives.* Edited by G. J. S. Govett. Amsterdam: Elsevier, 1976.

ZOHAIR, NAWAB, and KLAUS LÜCK. "Test Mining of Metalliferous Mud from the Red Sea Bottom." *Meerestechnik* 10, no. 6 (December 1979): 181–216.

||||| Sources |||||

Figures

1. no credit
2. Courtesy of Preussag AG
3. Source: R. H. Charlier, "Other Ocean Resources," *Ocean Yearbook,* 1978, p. 187
4. Source: Harald Bäcker, "Mineral Resources in Coast Areas," 1976
5. Courtesy NMU Cartographic Laboratory, 1979, © JLL
6. Courtesy of Shell and Esso
7. Courtesy of Arbeitsgemeinschaft Meerestechnischgewinnbare Rohstoffe, Federal Republic of Germany
8. Courtesy of Preussag AG
9. Courtesy of Preussag AG
10. Courtesy of Saudi-Sudanese Joint Red Sea Commission
11. Courtesy of Saudi-Sudanese Joint Red Sea Commission
12. Courtesy of Preussag AG
13. Courtesy of Preussag AG
14. Source: J. M. McRobie and D. Green, "Potash Extraction from the Dead Sea: A Summary," 1980, p. 12
15. Source: J. M. McRobie and D. Green, "Potash Extraction from the Dead Sea: A Summary," 1980, p. 12
16. Source: J. M. McRobie and D. Green, "Potash Extraction from the Dead Sea: A Summary," 1980, p. 11
17. Source: R. H. Charlier, "Other Ocean Resources," *Ocean Yearbook,* 1978, p. 166
18. Courtesy of S. H. Salter
19. no credit
20. Source: William E. Richards and Joseph R. Vadus, "Ocean Thermal Energy Conversion: Technology Development," *Marine Technology Journal,* February/March 1980, p. 11
21. Source: William E. Richards and Joseph R. Vadus, "Ocean Thermal Energy Conversion: Technology Development," *Marine Technology Journal,* February/March 1980, p. 11

Photographs

Atomic Energy of Canada, Ltd: page 36
British Petroleum Co., Ltd.: page 60
Elsevier: page 68
Max Ganado: pages 116–117
Government of Canada: page 112
National Geographic Society: page 97 (Dean Conger)
Preussag AG: frontispiece, pages 10–11, 16, 52, 54, 55, 100, 101, 102, 102–103
Red Sea Commission: page 99 (top)
Shell Oil Co.: page 56
Statoil: pages 49, 50–51
Woods Hole Oceanographic Institute: pages 12 (top: Robert D. Ballard; center: John Edmund; bottom: Fred Grassle), 13 (top: Robert Hessler), 35 (Dudley Foster), 98 (top and bottom: David Ross)
A.A.M. van der Heyden: page 104

⦚⦚⦚ Index ⦚⦚⦚

Hydrological studies, 107
Hydrophone, 65, 80
Hydrothermal activity, 46, 130, 132
Hydrothermal (metalliferous) mud, 24
Hydrothermal vents, 34

Iceland, shells in, 40, 44
Ilmenite, *14*, 31, 42
Incrustations, 45
INDAS (Integrated Navigation and Data-processing System), 95–96
India
 coal of, 44
 magnetite of, 44
 tidal ranges in, 124
Indian Ocean
 polymetallic nodules in, 25
 red clay in, 25
Indium, 119
Indonesia
 heavy-mineral sands of, 42
 tin of, 40, 44
Industrial sands, 23
Integrated Navigation and Data-processing System (INDAS), 95–96
International Marine Parks, 142
International Ocean-Space Institutions, 142
International Seabed Authority, *see* United Nations International Seabed Authority
Iodine, 119
Iridium, 108
Iron, 31
 location of, 46
 from minerals in sands, 42
 in nodules, 28
 in red clay, 25
 in sea water, 118, 119
Iron magnetite, 26
Iron ore, 25, 43
Iron sands, 41, 43
Ironstone, 23
Isaacs, John D., 118, 124, 132
Italy, coral of, 40

Japan
 coal mining of, 38, 44
 and continuous line bucket

system (CLB), 82
 heavy-mineral sands of, 42
 magnetite of, 44
 and nodule mining, 82
 research in, 33, 125
 sand and gravel of, 39
Japan Current, 126
Java, 42
Jordan River, 114

Karbe, Ludwig, 86
Kautiliya, *Arthasastra*, 114
Kebrit Deep, 92
Kelp, 127
Kennecott, 76

Land mining vs. sea mining, 30, 32, 33
Law of the Sea Convention, *see* United Nations Convention of the Law of the Sea
Laws of Oléron, 21
Lead
 classification of, 23
 location of, 46
 in muds, 91
 in nodules, 28
Lime, 31
Lime sands and shells, 23
Limestone, 23
Limonites, *10*
Limpets, 34
Linebaugh, Ruth, 42
Lingan Colliery (Cape Breton, Canada), 37–38
Lithium, 118, 119
Lobsters, copper in, 30
Lockheed Missiles and Space Company, 130
Loncarevic, Dr. B. D., 24
Louisiana, sulphur mining of, 45
Luzon, 42

Magnesia, 39
Magnesite, 31
Magnesium, 133
 as by-product of sea-salt mining, 115
 classification of, 23
 in nodules, 28

production value of, 43
 in red clay, 25
 salts, 118
 in sea water, 119
 sites for, 26
Magnetite, 31
 classification of, 23
 location of, 44
Magnetometry, 48
Malahoff, Alex, 46, 48, 130, 132
Malaysia, 44
Malta
 proposal to the U.N., 142
 salt pans, *116–117*
Manganese, 31
 location of, 44, 46
 nodules, 24, 26, 28, 30, 31, 43, *53*, 69, 73, 74, 77, 93–94, 137
 production of, 88
 in red clay, 25
 reserves of, 32
 in sea water, 119
 uses of, 88
Marginal mining, 39, 45–46
Marine-biological engineering, 120
Meadows, sea, 34
Mediterranean Sea, 22
 flora and fauna of, 113, 114
 manganese in, 44
 pollution of, 65
 Suez Canal effect on, 113
Mercury, 31
Mero, John, 32, 70, 74, 76
MESEDA (Metalliferous Sediments Atlantic II Deep), 92
MESEDA I, 93
MESEDA II, 93
MESEDA III, 93, 95
Metallic salts, 23
Metallic sulfides, 23
Metalliferous brines, 23
Metalliferous muds
 contents of, 23
 raising, from seabed, 93–94
 sites for, 24, 26
Metalliferous ooze, 31, 45
 contents of, 44
 location of, 24, 42, 44
Metals
 origin of, in the ocean, 24–25